T0171544

Time Out, Tune In, Turn On

Live the Path of Your Heart

LEENY THOMAS

BALBOA
PRESS
A DIVISION OF HAY HOUSE

Balboa Press books may be ordered through booksellers or by contacting:

Balboa Press
A Division of Hay House
1663 Liberty Drive
Bloomington, IN 47403
www.balboapress.com.au
1-(877) 407-4847

ISBN: 978-1-4525-0733-0 (sc)
ISBN: 978-1-4525-0737-8 (e)

Printed in the United States of America

Balboa Press rev. date: 10/15/2012

To my family.

With love and light,

we grow.

Table of Contents

About the Author

L eeny lives with her family on the Sunshine Coast in Queensland, Australia. She is a devoted mother and step-mum, and her family life is grounding and fulfilling. She takes pleasure in cooking, crafting, playing, and gardening every day.

In the 1990's, Leeny studied at the University of Queensland and graduated with degrees in Speech and Language Pathology, Molecular Biology, and Biochemistry.

Over the past eighteen years, Leeny has enriched the lives of people of all ages, across community, disability, education, and health settings. As a qualified speech and language pathologist, Leeny established a private clinical practice in Brisbane in 2001. She specialised in the field of disability and provided a range of services including assessment, therapy, programs, and training for people with complex communication needs and challenging behaviour.

Throughout her professional experience, Leeny found that her clients, and the people in their support networks, valued time with one another and enjoyable interaction as important components of a quality life.

Leeny invites the power of healing to guide and support her journey through life. She uses natural therapies and spiritual practices to cleanse and balance her mind, heart, and body. Leeny enjoys writing to release, heal, and teach.

To find out more about Leeny, please visit her website: leenythomas.com

Preface

Welcome. Thank you for inviting this book into your presence. I am excited about the possibility that you may embark on a journey of life change—to live the path of your heart. You have an adventurous itinerary in your hands and a welcoming landscape awaits you.

People in your everyday life will benefit from witnessing the new direction you take. Even fleeting encounters with your warm eyes and kind smile will arouse curiosity about your unique light, radiating from your open heart. Children in particular will experience comfort in your presence and will flourish in the goodness you share. Lives of young and old will blossom with you in creative ways.

My wish is that we support one-another to embrace everyday life change, for small steps lead to profound effects. I hope this book warms your heart and touches your soul.

In a snapshot, this book will offer you the opportunity to:

- Engage with easy-to-read, real-life stories.

- Learn a simple strategy to renew your being and reshape your life.

- Explore self-guided learning, healing, and growth.

- Create a lighter, brighter future for *you* and for *all*.

Background

I thought I was in control and had my life under control in the late '90s. I had three tertiary degrees, a long-term relationship, a private clinical practice, and a home of outstanding value. I was healthy, social, financially stable, and dedicated to my career in clinical practice. However, getting there was a long, tough road. I was far too hard on myself.

As the tenth year of my relationship with my partner approached in 2004, and he was still reluctant to formalise commitment through marriage, I put forward an ultimatum: "You either propose or I'll be on the go." I thought this would push him along! To this day, I still do not know if I would have had the courage to leave if he said, "No" or continued to do nothing. This is difficult for me to admit, but it is true.

One month later, my partner proposed and my picture was complete. Filled with satisfaction, I had no idea that our wedding would not eventuate. Within eighteen months, our relationship was over and it was his decision. At the time, it was not to my liking. My life collapsed—I was wounded by betrayal. I had invested heavily over the years to protect my vision of what I thought should have been the perfect plot: study, career, engagement, wedding, and then children. I set aside my longing for children to satisfy my belief that *children come after career and marriage*.

When my world crumbled, I fell apart. Amidst coping and grieving, I was broken and empty. Yet somehow, I took care to heal my heart and strengthen my resolve to make a fresh start. Upon finding my truth, I no longer desired to live in my old home or continue in private practice when I felt weak and alone.

Falling in love again was a treasured gift on Christmas Eve in 2006. Uniting with my new partner was completely unexpected. Mutual desire and sensitivity ignited our deep-soul connection and we created a loving, safe space for nurturing one-another with tender care. In the midst of this magic, it was logical and easy for me to honour the desires of my heart, so I closed my private practice and sold my old home.

My new partner already had a beautiful daughter, so in the case of my second loving relationship, children came before marriage! Our family home in the hinterland was our humble, peaceful retreat. Our love was blissful, our lives were enjoyable, and we were content in our quaint community. We lived in the moment. Blessed with love, we focussed on a fulfilling future. We did not envisage the arising of challenges and complications along *our* path. Looking back, we had major hurdles and potholes waiting for us!

We maintained a happy hive through family nurturing and loving commitment. Our deeply special events of marriage in 2008 and the birth of our beautiful son in 2009 infused our lives with celebration and joy in such trying times.

During our challenges over the last six years, we supported one-another to live true to our hearts. Yet, our journey has been incredibly testing, demanding, and depleting on all levels: emotionally, physically, spiritually, and financially. Like many, we lost our nest egg in the share market crash, brought property on a high and sold for a loss on the low, over-invested in family issues, and endured multiple relocations to accommodate the fleeting nature of my husband's casual work.

At the very least, we were determined to live our lives with love and integrity, even if the consequence was to live below the breadline. My husband supported my desire to be a full-time, breast-feeding mum despite our depleted financial situation. My decision to relinquish a well-paid professional career was an important step for me, to honour the desire of my heart. I did not expect to feel so vulnerable and burdened by guilt. I attempted to establish two different home-based businesses as an attempt to assist in rebuilding our finances whilst parenting full-time. However, the businesses were difficult to bring to fruition in a small community during such dire economic times.

We have only recently found higher ground. Now living on the coast, my husband has secured a full-time position in a job he enjoys, close to home. Our family is settled and our lives are smoothing out. I can now reflect on our journey and laugh with lightness—we are accustomed to welfare and living from op shops! At least I can now say this out loud, rather than stay silent and bow my head.

My decision to commit to full-time parenting still leaves me with a sense of something being unresolved: *Why do I find something I love and want to do so challenging at times?* The answer to this question feels beyond me so I have not tried to find it. I have gone about my life, doing the usual things I do, every day and have hoped that this niggling dilemma would go away.

I have however, started to do one thing new, and that is to write. Whilst writing is not new to me, it is a new activity for me to do in my role as a mother. I have written in personal journals during various stages of my life. In fact, I have filled many books and note pads, and placed them aside on a shelf or tucked them away to hide in the cupboard. Over the years, I discarded my writing amidst other bits and pieces in the process of clearing clutter and thought nothing further of it.

It is a lovely feeling to write freely in my journal, without the pressure of complying with theoretical terminology or set structures as required during my past roles of student, scientist, and speech pathologist. I enjoy writing and find it quiet satisfying. However, this time, there is something very different about my writing experience—I have decided to share!

The thought of sharing my innermost workings triggers a fluttery feeling in the narrow space between my tummy and my heart. Why is sharing what I write, such a big step for me?

The truth is, my writing shows who I *really* am. It is a tangible record of my unfiltered, honest thoughts and expressions of raw feeling, balanced with the gentle, sensitive, pure voice and intelligent wisdom of my heart. Therefore, if I were to lock my thoughts, feelings, and wise words away, I would not be writing this book with so much to say!

Time Out, Tune In, Turn On is the story of my everyday life change, as a parent and wife. I share with you, how I discovered this very simple strategy and applied it to survive, learn, heal, and grow in everyday life. In the "Heart-of-the-Moment Learning Resource" you are invited to explore my raw, real journal entries and reflections. You also have the opportunity to experiment with this strategy, write about your experiences, and reflect on your personal journey of learning, healing, and growth. Beads of desire and jewels of wise guidance will begin to rise from your heart. By applying *Time Out, Tune In, Turn On*, you will discover a gentle and effective way to renew your being and reshape your life!

Time Out, Tune In, Turn On has renewed my being and reshaped my life. I now enjoy parenting more than I ever have before. With balance and flexibility, I now embrace the dance of life and release my feelings freely. I now live joyfully and rest assured that I am loved and supported at all times, by my happy, whole heart!

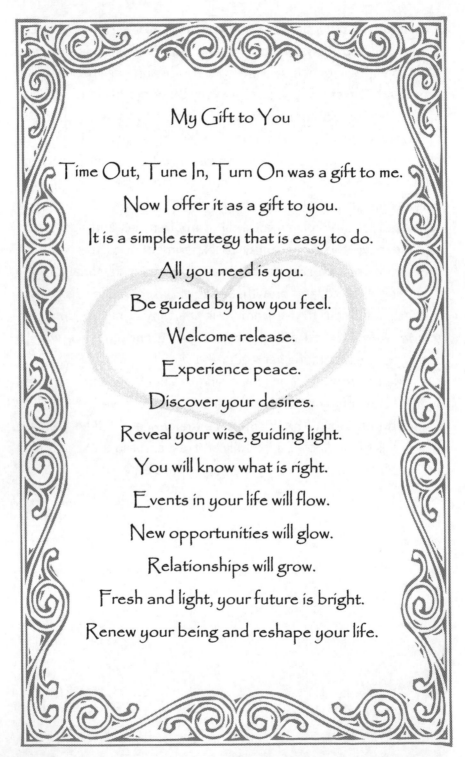

My Gift to You

Time Out, Tune In, Turn On was a gift to me.

Now I offer it as a gift to you.

It is a simple strategy that is easy to do.

All you need is you.

Be guided by how you feel.

Welcome release.

Experience peace.

Discover your desires.

Reveal your wise, guiding light.

You will know what is right.

Events in your life will flow.

New opportunities will glow.

Relationships will grow.

Fresh and light, your future is bright.

Renew your being and reshape your life.

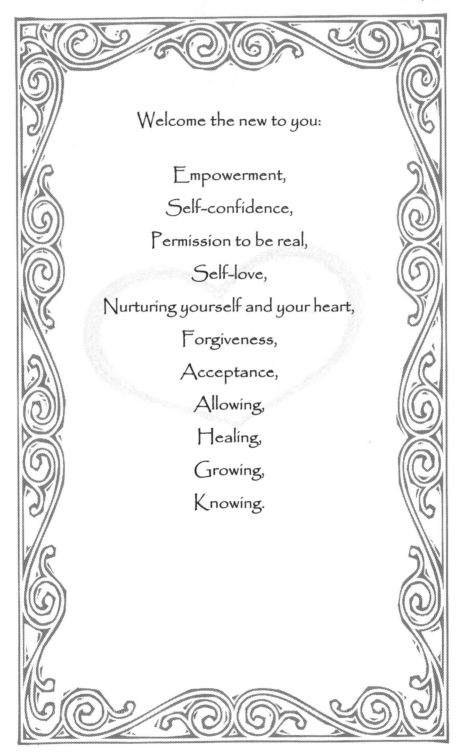

Welcome the new to you:

Empowerment,

Self-confidence,

Permission to be real,

Self-love,

Nurturing yourself and your heart,

Forgiveness,

Acceptance,

Allowing,

Healing,

Growing,

Knowing.

Chapter 1

Am I Normal?

I took great pride in being organised on school mornings. I had finished the lunches, the dishwasher was on, and the clothes were spinning in the machine. I only had to finish a few little things so I said in an upbeat tone, "Let's put our clothes on, polish our teeth, pack our bags, and off we go!" I thought to myself, *it is nice when everything flows!*

We were so close to making it through the door on time. I cannot recall what happened. Somehow, I found myself sitting at the dining room table, sipping plunger coffee—not because it was hot, but because I was making the most of what I had at the time, even if my coffee was cold! I knew on some level that the caffeine would do the trick!

In all honesty, feeling better afterward had more to do with getting out what I *really* had to say! This was my journal entry:

> Oh, my gosh! Am I normal? The hardest thing I have done in my life is parent and try to do it well!
>
> I thought birth was the hardest thing I would ever have to do as a parent!
>
> I surrendered myself to the universe—if I came through, it was meant to be.
>
> I thought I was going to have a home birth, with every detail etched and a grand visualisation of overall calm and relaxation. Wow, when I look back, we didn't even get the oil burner on! Birth was just full-on entrapment and surrender. Although it felt like eternity, it was only momentary. On the upside, my dire exhaustion was relieved with surgical intervention, and I could rest assured that I only have to go through the birthing experience again if I have another baby!

In giving birth, there was certainly no sagging and swaying of the ups and downs that go on in parenting, fluctuating day-by-day, hour-by-hour, and even minute-by-minute sometimes. This rocky ride is breaking me and I'm exhausted.

There are the good times and great moments—usually fits of laughter or overwhelming tears of joy when an unexpected, heart-warming moment occurs like, "Mummy, I just love you so much!" However, sneaky, creepy, sticky webs of entrapment keep finding their way into my life and causing strife!

I feel like retreating, curling up in a tiny cupboard as an attempt to hide and make the pain go away. However, when I am brave enough to venture out, the icky, sticky threads will still be there and I will have to pick my way through them with fine composure, so they do not constrict and trap me again.

The more I resist or try to reclaim control of my life, the more those threads thicken and multiply. Like twining three spun fibres into a yarn—singularly they pull apart with ease, yet together they hold firm and strong. Only a fully intended, divisive invention will cut them clean.

Perhaps antidepressants might do the trick—flat-line the bottoms and take the edge off the steep, sudden, plummeting valleys of my emotions; maybe even leave a little light on in the room. But would they take the edge off the thrilling highs, the complete joy, and the utter glee that comes from dancing naked to daggy tunes on the keyboard? Or singing full throttle with all sorts of screams as my little one flies off the lounge chair into a nest of cushions on the floor? Would they have nullified the in-the-moment adrenaline rush whilst wiping clean all prior recollections of pain?

I breathe and sigh, gather my will, and gently tease my way out through the web that looms outside the door. At any moment, self-doubt and self-pity make the fibres intensify and block out the light. In darkness there is no nurturing embrace, just silent suffocation. I know I have a strong desire to embrace life so I plead, "It's got to get easier than this!"

My eyes shut tight, teeth clench, and hands clasp my face. I breathe in with restriction and force the air out as I say to myself, "Back I go, back to, back on, back up, and back through." A bit like self-talk, mustering the courage to take the next step. Slowly, I soften and see a dim flicker of light beneath the tiring overlays of my pain. It gives me hope and I decide to make a change—to step up and step out, but not step back this time. I was sure of that.

As waves of light caress me with their gentle, warm glow, I feel support for my desire to create something different. "No, I'm not going back. I just can't do the pain again!" I state out loud, telling the world. It's a gratifying feeling to stand up and say no to this habitual pattern of pain. I am so glad I am here now, realising this and getting it off my chest.

Wise words from the voice of my heart speak with truth and simplicity: "There is another way." I look to the door and the web is gone. I feel myself taking a gentle breath like a soft piece of tissue catching the breeze. This is a nice change!

This moment has finally resolved—it was tricky at first, but now I am at ease. I thought I was living when I focused on industrious goals and achieved them, like studying full-time for eight years, while juggling various part-time jobs—quite often two at a time, or building a private clinical practice from the ground up.

The financial and material wows of my life are dormant at present, a polite way to say, "In dire despair." Yet, I am alive, and that I know! The simplest spark brings immense pleasure, like when my son says, "Brush my teeth, Mummy. No, I'll do it!" Or, "Mummy, I love you, and I forgive you!" even when I'm crouched over in child's pose, cheeks salty from tears, when there was no way out but to cry.

I hadn't laughed so much, so fully from my belly or reshaped so much in my body in the course of four years, until I reached motherhood. Yet, I am being stretched again, to reconsider what I want in my life. Why is parenting so hard at times? What is a meaningful occupation at this stage life for me?

I know deep down in my heart that parenting is for me, no matter how trying it can be, and re-evaluating where I want to be is okay. I am happy with my family, home, and garden, and will continue to make the most of what I have.

I have reached a humble realisation and affirmation, that parenting is a true, good, loving work role. I do get weak and doubtful though. I am learning to develop my self-assurance and acceptance that parenting is indeed, an essential and important role, even if only for my family and me.

After writing at the table with my cold coffee, the house was quiet and still. I closed my journal and soaked up the sound and sensation of the little "click" as I gently pressed the snap-lock button. I felt much better, left my journal on the table, and moved into a new cycle in my everyday life.

I packed the bags, picked up the keys, kissed our puppy goodbye, and greeted the children with a soothing smile. Changing my son out of his pyjamas and polishing his teeth were no longer a necessity. His big sister was ready. I closed the front door. We meandered along the garden path, out through the gate, and settled into the car. Not a single word was spoken—we were peaceful and content.

When I came home later that day, I saw my journal on the table and instead of placing it back onto the shelf in the dining room, where it once sat collecting dust, I moved it to my bedroom. I placed it up high on a shelf to hide well away from easy reach. My body let out a sigh and for a moment, I closed my eyes. I stood still and wondered, *what happened to me this morning?* This question had me beat and I was glad the ordeal was over. I shook my head and slowly walked away. A little voice tiptoed behind me whispering, "Am I normal? Do I need some kind of help?"

Chapter 2

Dawning

Sitting at the table and writing, while sipping my cold coffee, was a quick way to cool-off from the heat of an explosive situation. The relief was not as immediate as jumping into a pool or spritzing my face, but it was very effective and deeply significant. I returned to my life refreshed and the events in my life thereafter, flowed. There was no nagging, pleading, pushing, or overdoing. This was a welcome change. When we were all in the car and I was about to set the gear in reverse, I decided that I was going to sit down and write more often, whenever I felt I needed to.

I seemed to be waiting for my life to eventually smooth out, yet every day was greeting me with chaos and stress. Many small, yet volatile events were landing on *my* plate, ready to burn in any direction I turned. I was frustrated with constantly having to face challenges and heated situations. I felt depleted and could no longer push on. I was consuming so much energy by trying to keep my life and myself together.

A number of months had passed since I had written my journal entry, "Am I Normal?" I was writing more and did not realise that I was feeling better overall. One afternoon, my husband reached out and whisked me into his arms. He nuzzled into my neck and warmly whispered, "I can see you're changing. I like it and it's helping our family harmony." His generous, tender compliment softened my body and caressed my soul. I had forgotten how much I had evolved.

Upon receiving his gentle reassurance, I felt the sparkle of a happier, more confident me. The excitement about my change bubbled away freely and I suddenly burst out loud, "Would you like to read some of my writing since it is having such good effect on me?" Soon after, my fizzy freedom smoothed out and I wished I had kept a grip on my excitement as part of me wanted to contain my deep, dormant self-revelations. This was a side of my personality that I did not want my husband did not see!

With an air of apprehension, I handed my journal to my husband that night and I could not let him or my book of secrets out of sight. I busied myself whilst casting a careful eye in his direction. He made no comments or noticeable expressions. When my husband was finished reading, he said simply and honestly, in a tone flecked with surprise, "Your writing is a skill I haven't recognised!" He elaborated, "You should share what you write more often."

I felt a lifting sensation from the base of my brain, just as you pry a weed from the ground—initially, a short firm tug and then a sturdy, gentle, persuasive pull to ensure the network of capillary roots release their sturdy hold. My weed of shame was free. Sunshine tickled the vacant space and hinted at a new possibility—if another person was interested in my writing and could identify with what I was writing about, then perhaps I was normal after all!

I needed validation and was happy to leave our intimate experience of sharing at that. I was not yet convinced that my writing was worthy of public sharing and I had not yet considered, that sharing my writing could be in my destiny. Writing was natural but sharing was *new*.

The dazzling exchange with my husband that evening ignited a strange, new feeling within me. I was now curious about how I evolved and how my life change began to unfold. Therefore, I decided to read my writing to see if it would reveal what was going on inside me. This was new territory.

At the time of writing, I had not intended to return to read. My intention was to write as I felt I needed to, at the time, and leave it at that. Journal writing for me was about getting it out and letting it be, putting it away and eventually, throwing it away someday.

When read "Am I Normal?" I witnessed myself embark on, and complete, a complex inner journey. I was thankful that I recorded my experience that day so truthfully. I knew that I needed to take my time to reflect on this event more deeply.

I did not like reading my written material initially—it was a little bit dark and scary. I felt embarrassed about rambling and was ashamed about the existence and nature my pain. I needed time to accept my honest reality. I was surprised with my ability to transform my inner turmoil and emerge centred, peaceful, and refreshed. This turn around had me intrigued—something was going on whilst I was writing, that was helping me.

Over the next few weeks, I reflected upon this revealing event and wondered: How did this experience bring about a change in my everyday life?

A dull, firm drumbeat looming in the distance was beginning to intensify. As I contemplated this question, my answer was not yet complete—it was only dawning.

Chapter 3

Taking Space

W hen I found myself suddenly caught in an escalating, heated situation, I decided to take solo space. I removed myself from the situation and found a place to be alone. I walked into the dining room as it was close by and sat down at the table. I did not have to go behind closed doors for privacy—somehow there was an air of mutual respect for one-another's space. The environment around me was still and calm. I was not even interrupted by our dog wanting to play ball.

I unplugged from the stress and left the chaos behind. I changed an old habit of pushing through tough times. I did not unleash or contribute to the fireworks, or linger for a scolding. By removing myself from the heated situation, I took *time out*.

Time out is not a new concept for most people. It is a normal act and healthy strategy. Most of us take time out from time-to-time. Some of us take time out often and some of us do not take time out for ourselves at all. Taking time out from a heated situation, fuelled by escalating stress, chaos, and explosive reactivity however, is a new healthy concept for me.

In heated situations, I have usually tried to "survive the heat" by persisting and by putting up a shield to deflect harsh outbursts and protect my inner vulnerability. I thought this was all that I could do, and that it was important to stay grounded in this troublesome space if I was to contribute to resolution.

I denied the obvious—persisting and shielding were unhealthy habits. I settled for the belief that, *I had to maintain composure, even if I would feel uneasy and put myself under pressure to do so*. Therefore, I supressed my survival instincts and endured the consequences of many, varied tests. I would try to maintain composure and impose an illusion of control with a domineering voice and firm words. But, my cloak of composure would eventually rip at the seams from the intensity of my uncontrollable emotional outburst.

Taking time out this particular day was something that *just happened*. It was a quick, easy, and effective step. I was not fully aware of what I was doing, as this was not something that I had planned to do. Leaving the heated situation was like reaching for a helping hand with a ray of hope that I would experience a better feeling in doing something new.

I left the heart of a heated situation and took the first step in a new direction. I did not realise in this instance, that *time out* would become the first step of my survival strategy.

By taking time out,
I removed myself from an unhealthy situation.
I gave myself time and space to experience a new way.

Chapter 4

Letting Out and Letting Go

I n a quiet, private space, I reached for my journal and let out all that I needed to say. I let my inner voice speak freely as my writing ran wild. My unfiltered thoughts poured out—I had so much to say. I could not put my feelings into words at the time. I was not able to label my emotions or even able to acknowledge that I was experiencing pain.

I found myself embarking on a vivid, visual tour of my painful feelings in action, guided through my own sense of what I needed to do. I instinctively used imagery to describe the nature and pattern of my pain and the hold it had on me. I was bound in a sneaky, creepy, sticky web.

Whilst I was sitting at the table writing, my visualisation experience slowly uncovered my pain. I saw myself crouching in a cupboard. I was not able to admit how entrapped my inner feelings were but I was able to describe how I felt physically: "My eyes shut tight, teeth clench, and hands clasp my face. I breathe in with restriction and force the air out." Somehow, the visual description of my constricting body was enough to trigger release and create a shift in my painful reality. I felt my tension dissolve and my physical body soften. I also saw my body relax and release in my visual scene. I no longer had to contain the anguish and turmoil of my pain. Stillness filtered through my being and aligned with my calm surround. This was a blissful experience!

By expressing my thoughts and experiencing my pain, I *let out* all that I needed to, privately, in a way that was natural for me. By revealing my painful, raw inner reality, I *let go* and experienced immediate relief. Everything I wanted to say, experience, and acknowledge was vented completely, honestly, and privately.

I tuned-in to my thoughts and emotions as they were active, in full manifest, and expressed them as I needed to, with the resources I had at the time. By taking time out in the heart of a heated situation,

I gave myself time and space to tune in—to release my inner reality and experience relief.

I did not put my inner world in a box to open up with my husband that evening, or to float away in a relaxing bath. I did not put my inner world into a pot to simmer on the stovetop and serve for dessert to digest all over again. I did not put up a shield of resistance to contain my feelings of frustration and tension. I did not explode full throttle or lash out with harsh accusations, to later feel burdened by the weight of embarrassment and guilt. There was no thinking, no planning, and no asking.

My tune-in process was about experiencing and expressing as I needed to, in a way that was spontaneous and natural for me, using the resources I had at hand. Visualisation and writing were my methods for release. My welcome gift was relief.

I was perplexed. This was an interesting way that I could set my pain free! I set it free from my physical body, and free from being a concealed, inner entity. It seemed like someone was listening to me, but who could this be? I finally took responsibility to listen to the *real* me.

I awakened to how I coped with my pain in action, during my tune-in experience. The "old me" did not want to see or feel my pain; it was happy to hide my pain and avoid facing it, for fear that it was too scary and overbearing. The "old me" had mastered the art of supressing my pain with the disguise of self-protection. I did not realise I was denying the existence and honesty of my real feelings, and that it would be healthy for me to express myself freely. The old me feared I would not be able to cope if I let my guard down and admitted my emotional reality.

I also awakened to my pain being its own entity, and that it wanted to go on and have its own way with me. My pain grew stronger the longer it remained undetected. It was content for me to push through feelings of stress and frustration, and the complications of everyday, heated situations. My pain fed on my pattern of resistance.

Through the tune-in process, I discovered the existence of my pain and released the hold it had on me. This fuelled my desire to experience a *new* reality—I did not want to return to a life of pain!

Throughout my past, I thought I had addressed my issues with pain quite adequately, for I was well accustomed to stress management and relaxation strategies. I practised yoga, relaxation, and meditation with interest, discipline, and regularity. I looked forward to my weekly sessions to experience much needed serenity and tranquillity.

I attended sessions in a studio with natural surrounds, a warm blanket, comfortable mat, candles, incense, and soft, soothing music. A gentle voice would guide me through an indulgent, peaceful session and nudge me back into reality if I fell asleep.

Whilst formal sessions have been an invaluable component of cultivating a balanced, healthy life, they occurred at a time and place that were separate to the situations in which my feelings of pressure and unease would arise.

Observing my pain and experiencing its release during my tune-in process occurred in the *heart* of a heated situation, on the day I sat with my cold coffee. This process did not occur during a session that was scheduled, attended, or paid for. My tune-in process was done in the *heart-of-the-moment*. I did not need to schedule a session or depend on particular materials, people, or resources. I did as I needed to do in the heart-of-the-moment and used what I had at hand.

By tuning-in, I discovered that I did not have to put my thoughts or feelings on hold, or spend valuable energy on maintaining composure. My painful inner reality was vented and cleared in the heart of a heated moment, honestly and privately.

Giving myself time and space to express, release, and feel relief was the second step in my new life experience. I did not realise at the time, that *tune in* would be the second step of my survival strategy.

By tuning-in,
I experienced and expressed my raw, inner
reality, honestly, completely, and privately.
Release offered welcome relief.

Chapter 5

Connecting
Within

After release, I experienced welcome relief. I was in a calm, quiet space. I resonated with a sensation of stillness and melted into the soft sanctuary of my heart. I did not realise what was happening. The process of connecting with my heart was a natural nesting instinct. I rested here for some time, with ease, and enjoyed my feeling of peace.

Illuminated with a gentle, golden glow, the inner world of my heart was filled with warmth, nurturing, and surreal sensitivity. I had *connected within*. My inner light was shining free from tiring layers of pain and long-term neglect. I was held in comfortable embrace, safe and secure in this loving, sacred space. I felt blessed to experience this magnificent opportunity.

When I connected within, I saw the inner light of my heart turn on. It was like I flicked a switch. I experienced a new way of being that was much more desirable. I wanted to experience this golden glow and the feeling of being enveloped in warm, tender-loving care more frequently in my life. It was also my heart's desire to linger in this moment together, for a little while. My desire to create a different life experience—a life that was graceful and flowing, began to climb its way through the golden light.

In a space of love, I decided that I did not want to go back to my pain. I created a shift by honouring my desire for a new life experience, as it sprouted from the fertile source of my heart.

I experienced a deep sense of inner knowing that this decision was a necessary and timely step for me. My heart's intelligence and wisdom was guiding and reassuring me, "*There is another way.*" I did not have the details or hatch a plan, but I experienced a sure sense of knowing that I would be okay. This was a welcome change.

I was grateful for having rested in the sacred space of my heart, to listen and observe, rather than swiftly return to my life. I experienced peace and emerged refreshed, knowing that I was okay. During this magical reconnection, I felt reassurance and support from my heart.

In loving, safe space, I was able to open-up to the creation of a new life experience, in my own time and in my own way.

This was a new way of being for me. I discovered a stunning inner treasure—my warm, wise, loving heart; the source of my true desires. A precious relationship with my heart was re-ignited. Together, we were able to offer one another vital nurturing and support.

Re-igniting a relationship with my heart was the third step in my new life experience. I did not realise at the time that *turn on* would become the third step of my survival strategy.

By turning-on,
I renewed a loving relationship with my heart.
My inner wisdom and true desires were illuminated.
I felt at peace and emerged refreshed.

Chapter 6

Surviving

After writing in my journal on the day I wondered if I was normal, I experienced peace. I felt refreshed and was able to move on with my life in a pleasant way. I closed the door behind me and meandered along the garden path with the children, feeling grounded and centred. Once we were seated in the car, I compassionately reassured myself that I would do the same thing again, when I felt the need to.

My life continued to be full and busy and I did not consider stopping to take a closer look at what I was doing, or what was happening to me. When my husband noticed that I was changing and our family harmony was improving, I decided to read my writing and reflect on what was going on in my life.

Whilst reading my journal entry, "Am I Normal?" I witnessed the release of my inner reality. It shifted from being concealed in darkness, to having all facets shine in the light. I experienced a gradual dawning of a simple, yet powerful strategy. This strategy helped me cool-off quickly from the heat.

Time Out, Tune In, Turn On emerged as my unique *survival strategy*. It was easy to do and had three simple steps:

Step 1
Time Out
Take solo space

Step 2
Tune In
Let out and let go

Step 3
Turn On
Connect Within

When taking the first step in
doing something new,
trust that you will be guided through.

Step 1: Time Out

Taking time out is simple. You need to leave the situation in the *heart* of a heated moment and take solo space—a moment for yourself in a quiet, private space. You may simply leave the situation without saying anything, or you may choose to say what you need. With practise over time, you may be able to take a moment for yourself whilst you stay within the situation.

Taking time out will become a natural, automatic action the more you practise. Be kind on yourself and take time out when and where it suits you, as it naturally flows for you at the time.

My everyday environment was our family home. This was the perfect place for me to take time out initially. I was familiar with this environment and had quick, easy access to a range of comfortable, quiet, private spaces. The dining room was a central retreat, my bedroom offered much needed privacy, and various places in my garden offered nurturing and open space. I decided to ride out challenges when I encountered them in public if I had my son with me at the time.

As I became familiar with the process of taking time-out, I was able to start taking time out publically. With practise, I developed confidence in using a flexible approach for decision-making in the community. If I sensed that a problematic situation was going to arise, I would attempt to sail away as swiftly and gracefully as possible, even with my son in hand. When I was with my family in public, walking away a short distance was enough to give me a moment for solo space. This was particularly useful if I was sensitive to other people's comments.

Time out should not be dramatic or difficult. Don't *try* to take time out or overthink how to go about it. It is preferable to take time out when it spontaneously occurs and naturally flows for you.

Begin by taking time out in a familiar environment. Identify a quiet, comfortable place where you know you can take solo space. The first time I took time out from a heated situation was the biggest step to complete. The rest took care of itself!

Take time out.
Give yourself a gift of time and space.

Time Out

Take solo space.
Have a moment to yourself.
Breathe and simply be.

To be real, we must feel.

Step 2: Tune In

The tune-in process enabled me to release my thoughts and feelings in a way that I needed to, and with the resources that I had at the time. I experienced relief and could relax within minutes of feeling pressure and unease. I discovered that writing can be used as a powerful method of release after taking time out from a very challenging situation.

I have used a range of simple methods for releasing in the heart of a heated moment. These methods do not require materials, people, appointments, or financial resources: breathing, yawning, sighing, bouncing, tapping, stretching, swinging, humming, singing, dancing, and shaking. I have experienced the beneficial effects of release by tuning-in to my body and doing as I am guided to do instinctively, using my body's wisdom and feedback from physical levels of comfort and discomfort. I have also experienced releasing through artistic methods such as colouring, scribbling, drawing, sculpting, and sewing, if I have had access to the materials and felt the desire to use them.

My tune-in process was visualisation and writing on the day I sat at the table with my cold coffee. Visualisation enabled me to observe what my pain was doing to me and experience its release. Writing provided an outlet for my thoughts and emotions as they emerged. I felt *real* through complete, honest expression. I felt relieved through release of my pain.

Tune in to express and release.
Use what you have access to at the time.
Feel real.

Tune In

I love that my writing makes me laugh. I need not be concerned with what it does to others, because laughing gives me great service and even greater service I can give. We have all heard, "Lighten-up," "Be joyful," and "Just be." I've struggled with these concepts—found them short lived, usually nudged back into the humdrum patterns of the day, the job list, or dramas occurring with other people. Through writing, I am learning to focus my attention back onto myself and create space for myself in the here and now. It is helping and I am noticing change.

Tune In

Let out and let go.
Release all that you need to, privately.
Feel real and experience relief.

In light, I am able to be of service.

Step 3: Turn On

The turn-on process united me with the centre of my heart. After tuning-in and releasing, I felt much better and I could have returned to my life. However, by giving myself time to nest in the safe space of my heart and rest at ease with a feeling of peace, I discovered a deeper world of serenity and tranquillity.

The warm, golden glow of my heart was nurturing. A reciprocal relationship with my heart was re-ignited through mutual care and attention. My heart was a magnificent world of beauty and a comforting source of love, wisdom, *true* desire, assurance, and support.

Turning-on was a natural and relatively quick process for me to complete after I tuned-in to release. This was a surprise, for I had practised meditation in the past, which required a greater length of time to prepare the mind and relax the body, before centring in the heart.

When I connected with the warm, safe space of my heart, it was natural for me to rest and experience the beauty of this sacred place. For the first time in a long time, I was able to feel what I *really* desired. I was offered support, reassurance, and wise guidance. To reach my heart, all I needed to do was give myself time and space to release and then allow the process of connection to occur in its way and own time.

I did not need to worry about the heated situation, think of a way to solve it, or craft a plan for how to return to my day. The challenge, unease, and discontent from the situation miraculously dissolved by the time I completed my turn-on process. I emerged refreshed, knowing that I would go on with my life in alignment with what was important to me—a feeling of gracefulness, sensitivity, and peace. Somehow, the events in my life thereafter, flowed. What concerned me before, no longer bothered me now.

Turn on to re-ignite a loving
relationship with your heart.

Turn On

There is so much more to ourselves than we realise, or allow ourselves to experience, when we live busy lives. When we turn on, we receive the treasures of our heart, which sparkle with potential and possibility. We experience gentle, loving reassurance and are reminded to trust in ourselves, and in the world around us.

Turn On

Connect within.

Rest in the safe space of your heart.

Experience peace, nurturing, and support.

Observe the arising of your heart's desires.

Trust your heart's wise guidance.

Emerge refreshed.

When I know in my heart what is true,
I can ask for what I need, rather than
try to get by, or push through.
I feel fulfilled.

Summary:

I discovered *Time Out, Tune In, Turn On* as my survival strategy. It helped me cool-off quickly, from the heat of a challenging situation. I took time out, released what I needed to, and connected with my heart. This survival strategy enabled me to create a new, pleasant experience—I felt refreshed and was able to move on with my life in peace.

More and more people are learning to connect with their heart through scheduled relaxation and meditation. These practices are an important foundation for living a balanced life. However, *Time Out, Tune In, Turn On* is a strategy that can be applied in the *heart-of-the-moment*, as challenging situations arise in everyday life.

Time out provides much needed space to allow ourselves to tune in. By letting out and letting go, we allow ourselves to experience and express our raw, inner reality, as it is "in the moment." We are able to release our thoughts, emotions, and pain to experience relief instantaneously. By turning-on, we reignite a loving, nourishing relationship with our precious heart. We open-up to discovering our true desires and receiving wise inner guidance. We emerge from this process feeling refreshed. With clarity, we can move forward with our life; our decisions and actions are founded in love and peace.

By applying Time Out, Tune In, Turn
On, you will develop a new, healthy
relationship with your heart.
With care and attention, your heart will
reveal your truth, and guide you with loving
light, through a peaceful and fulfilling life.

Chapter 7

Learning, Healing, and Growing

After I discovered *Time Out, Tune In, Turn On* as my survival strategy, I was naturally curious . . . Was I applying this strategy in other everyday experiences? What was I writing about in my journal? Our lives are so full and busy, we can forget to take a closer look at what is going on. We can easily overlook how our everyday experiences are influenced by the choices we make.

Going back over my writing was like opening a sealed box of treasure. I revealed what I was experiencing and who I was becoming. I discovered that I was changing and so was my life. Over time, I noticed that I was feeling much better, my life was improving, and I wasn't so frequently experiencing strife!

I wondered about what was happening to me . . . How was I evolving? How was my life reshaping? I originally thought that I left the heart of a heated situation to survive, but breathing, venting, releasing, and connecting was helping me do more than revive.

When I reflected upon my various journal entries, I discovered that *Time Out, Tune In, Turn On* was a strategy that helped me do more than merely *survive*. I was learning, healing, and growing in everyday life!

As soon as I took time out and left an unhealthy situation, I created a new experience for myself. I instinctively called on my inner courage and realised that I had enough confidence to take a step in a new direction. The more I practised taking time out, the better I felt. Over time, I was empowered to own the cause-effect relationship in my life. I gradually reached acceptance that I was the only one responsible for creating new experience in my life.

By tuning-in to release, I learnt that it is normal and healthy for me to express my feelings, emotions, and thoughts as they emerged, raw and real, in the heart-of-the-moment, without being judged or disturbed. I no longer needed to cling to control to keep a lid on my life. I learnt that I was resourceful in my coping ability and that I was putting in too much effort trying to conceal my pain. I no longer needed to drape myself in a cloak of composure or continue to live under the pressure that was shutting me down.

I healed by acknowledging and releasing my pain and the hold it had on my life. By expressing my inner reality "in-the-moment", I finally felt *alive*! By shedding my emotional baggage and heavy weight of guilt and shame, I was no longer bogged in muddy mess of daily complications. My healing during the tune-in process was incredibly relieving. I gave myself soothing permission to express myself completely and privately, and mend my painful wounds.

By turning-on, I felt support and guidance from my loving, wise heart. Our precious relationship was reignited. With care and attention, we became whole. Connecting with the sacred space of my heart was a mutually nurturing experience. I realised that my heart and I had a need for attention too. My *real* desires began to rise and as I followed my heart's advice I began to sprout new growth. I started taking better care of myself and my surrounds. I was smiling more—inside and out!

By reigniting a loving relationship with my heart, I began to renew my being and reshape my life. I realised that I was growing as a person and changing my life when I began to experience feelings such as ease, peace, contentment, connectedness, and clarity. I began to follow my *true* desires without hesitation or dwelling. I experienced what it was like to feel light and happy, and to spontaneously embrace the dance of life. I flirted with feeling joyful and carefree whilst remaining centred in my being. I began to access the wonderment of my inner child and could now see so much beauty, vibrancy, and magnificence in the world around me! This was new for me to experience amidst the duties of my active, everyday life.

Through the process of learning,
healing, and growing,
I opened a new gateway and discovered that
I could live the path of my heart!

Live the path of your heart.

Learn

Heal

Grow

Live

Honour your desires.

Trust your heart to be your guide.

Sail with the flow of life.

Set healthy boundaries.

Give yourself permission to be real.

Embrace the light of life.

Feel alive.

Live joyfully.

Light of Life

Igniting our inner light is the essence of living a brighter, joyful life. By connecting with our heart, we discover our true desires, strengthen our inner knowing, forgive ourselves, rediscover self-love, and experience fulfilment. We develop confidence in knowing what we really need and become empowered to live in alignment with the desires and wisdom of our heart. We chart the course of our life, free from the shackles of painful patterns, and habits of resistance and reactivity.

During my turn-on process, I discovered that a busy inner alchemy of learning, healing, and growing was taking place. This wasn't something that I *tried* to do. Learning, healing, and growing occurred gradually and naturally.

In each instance I used *Time Out, Tune In, Turn On*, I began to renew on an emotional and physical level, and my life started to change shape. I would learn something new, discover new desires, and receive new guidance if I needed it at the time. Swift chemistry was occurring inside my heart. My learning, healing, and growth occurred in a timely manner. It was also practical and relevant to my everyday situation. However, my learning, healing, and growth could not be predicted or prescribed. I could not predict what I was going to learn, or how I would heal and grow. I could neither prescribe a formula to outline the lessons and healings that were occurring in my life.

Whilst *Time Out, Tune In, Turn On* was a simple three-step strategy, the processes that occurred during each step were *self-guided,* in the heart-of-the-moment. I discovered *Time Out, Tune In, Turn On* as a survival strategy initially. However, over time, I realised on a deeper level, that *Time Out, Tune In, Turn On* was a strategy for self-guided learning, healing, and personal growth.

I was delighted to discover that my learning, healing, and growth was self-guided. I was not told when to take time out or where to go. I was not told how to tune in or what to release. The arising of desires and guidance from my heart occurred if it was relevant at the time. I did not try to do anything in particular. I did not have any plans. I focussed on taking a moment for myself, releasing as I needed to, and resting in the sacred space of my heart. My self-guided learning, healing, and growth bubbled away on its own accord—I simply provided the time and space.

Sometimes I was aware that I was learning something new, healing a wound, and growing as a person. Other times, it was only after I reflected on my writing, that I came to understand how *Time Out, Tune In, Turn On* was renewing my being and reshaping my life.

My learning, healing, and growth meandered through issues related to control, forgiveness, self-love, self-care, and integrity. I experienced the emergence of new qualities in my everyday life such as compassion, acceptance, allowing, freedom, spontaneity, surprise, creativity, and playfulness. I nurtured the sprouting of dormant personal qualities such as self-responsibility, inner-courage, self-confidence, and empowerment.

I was now living a lighter, brighter life, in alignment with the path of my heart. I was setting healthy boundaries with people and when planning my schedule. I was gracefully embracing challenges and spontaneous surprises. I was nourishing my body and my heart. I was also beginning to share mutual sensitivity and creativity in some social relationships.

While there were no secret ingredients or magic formulas, a busy inner alchemy bubbled away inside my heart when I applied *Time Out, Tune In, Turn On*. Self-guided learning, healing, and growth was possible and effective, at any time, if I gave myself space and time to connect with the sacred centre of my loving, wise heart! This process was responsible for renewing my being and reshaping my life.

> Time Out, Tune In, Turn On was a simple
> strategy with a profound effect—over time,
> I renewed my being and reshaped my life!

Renew your being and
reshape your life!

Art of Living

It is a new art to live with comfort, moment-by-moment in our busy lives and in such tumultuous times. I now use Time Out, Tune In, Turn On to live a lighter, flowing life, in alignment with the path of my heart. In the sacred space of my heart, I discover what I need and trust the wise guidance I receive. My learning, healing, and growth is self-guided. I now live a new way of life. I have no grand plans. I walk slowly, self-assured in my ability to open my heart, flow with life, and flourish by embracing the abundant offerings that greet me along my way.

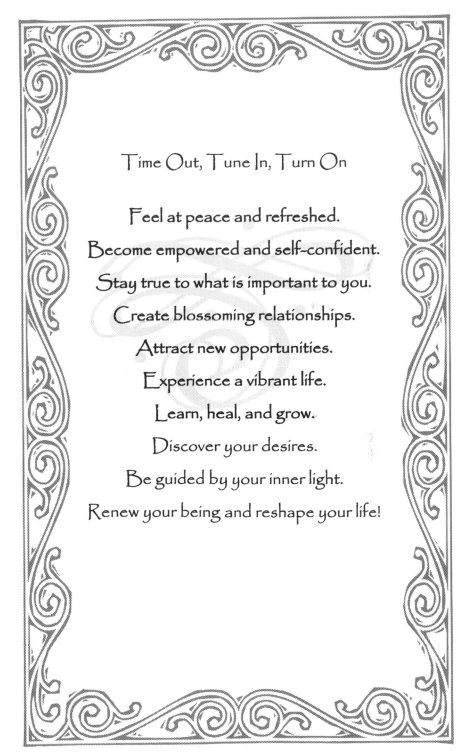

Time Out, Tune In, Turn On

Feel at peace and refreshed.

Become empowered and self-confident.

Stay true to what is important to you.

Create blossoming relationships.

Attract new opportunities.

Experience a vibrant life.

Learn, heal, and grow.

Discover your desires.

Be guided by your inner light.

Renew your being and reshape your life!

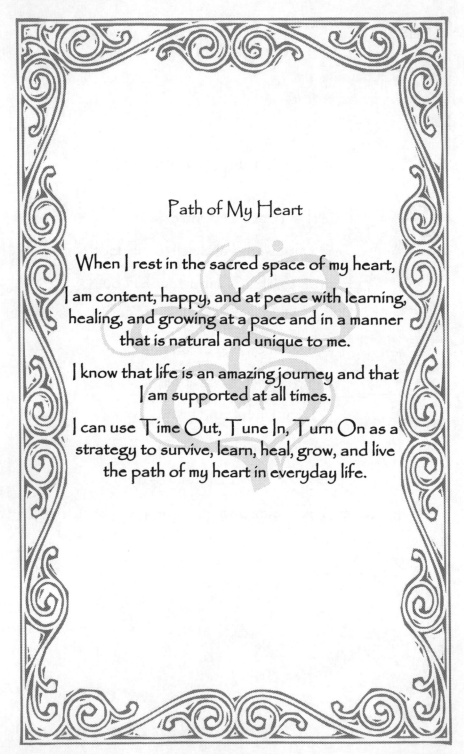

Path of My Heart

When I rest in the sacred space of my heart,

I am content, happy, and at peace with learning, healing, and growing at a pace and in a manner that is natural and unique to me.

I know that life is an amazing journey and that I am supported at all times.

I can use Time Out, Tune In, Turn On as a strategy to survive, learn, heal, grow, and live the path of my heart in everyday life.

Summary:

My everyday life was becoming enjoyable—I was growing as a person and feeling fulfilled in my life. My changes could have been easily overlooked as they were small and they gradually evolved. Overall, my personal growth and life change experience was self-guided. *Time Out, Tune In, Turn On* was the strategy that propelled me forward. *Time Out, Tune In, Turn On* was a simple strategy with a profound effect—it renewed my being and reshaped my life. I created a new way of experiencing life, from *living the path of my heart!*

Time Out, Tune In, Turn On can do more for you, than only helping you survive a trying time. *Time Out, Tune In, Turn On* will enable you to experience self-guided learning, healing, and growth in a way that is unique to you, as you live the path of your heart.

The practice of living the path of your
heart is a beautiful gift to give yourself.
This practice is uniquely special to you.

Chapter 8

Versatility

When I look back on the day I sat at the table to write with my cold coffee, I used *Time Out, Tune In, Turn On* to survive. I left the heat of a challenging everyday life situation to sit, breathe, vent, release, connect, and revive. I experienced a beneficial effect on my life immediately, and I decided that I would sit and write whenever I needed to cling to something to survive. *Time Out, Tune In, Turn On* became my new habit, my new survival instinct.

By writing about my experiences and reviewing them, I was able to reflect on my journey. I was evolving, my life was reshaping, and the way I was applying *Time Out, Tune In, Turn On* was changing too. This was not something I was trying to do, it was occurring gradually and naturally. I was my own guide.

I was beginning to "beat the heat" and was not so frequently experiencing strife. The heated situations which once ripped into a roaring fire, were now content to smoulder and smoke. They were reducing in intensity and I did not need to cool-off or calm-down so frequently. I learnt that I could apply *Time Out, Tune In, Turn On* in more ways, than to simply survive.

Whilst I could handle a little discomfort and unease in my life, I still found myself using *Time Out, Tune In, Turn On* to breathe, vent, release, connect, and revive. I no longer needed to leave a situation to take time out in a private space. I could now stay present in the situation and apply *Time Out, Tune In, Turn On* in the heart-of-the-moment.

This was a significant shift. I could take time out while I was sitting, standing, kneeling, or walking. Sometimes, I gestured with my hand and said to my son, "I need to take a moment." I would tune in and release all that I needed to, using the flow of my breath. I would breathe in through my nose and out through my mouth silently, for as long as I needed to, as my tension dissolved. The unsettled forces of the situation would simultaneously dissipate. On these occasions, I was not able to write and if I wanted to, I would write to record my experience another time.

Time Out, Tune In, Turn On became a new healthy habit in my life. I continued to apply this strategy regularly, even though my life was improving. I also found that I began to apply *Time Out, Tune In, Turn On* it in the heart of *any* moment. I was guided by my instinct and discovered that *Time Out, Tune In, Turn On* is a strategy which offers the benefit of *versatility*.

Heightened Awareness & Compassionate Acceptance

By tuning-in to how I was feeling, I lived with heightened awareness of the people, activities, and energies around me. I was able to detect emerging challenges or potential difficulties with enough time to divert around them or discern how to invest my attention and energy, whilst maintaining a healthy boundary. I lived with clarity about my role and was able to better balance duties with desired activities.

I was empowered to stay true to what I needed to do, rather than being swooped into the whirl of unexpected, distracting, and consuming events. I was able to detach from issues which were of no real concern to me, rather than hook into the temptation of judgement, and the opportunity to exercise influence or control. I was able to compassionately accept the busy hive of people and activities around me, and began to offer space for people and events to *be*. I no longer needed to remove myself or put myself into a bubble to shut off from my immediate surrounds.

I was now feeling lighter, living *in-tune* with my body, and flowing with the world around me. I was empowered to stay alert and attentive, with heightened awareness and acceptance of the natural divinity around me. I could now surrender to the fact that challenges would *always arise* and I was to choose *how* to experience them.

Gratitude & Blessing

I began to apply *Time Out, Tune In, Turn On* in the heart of happy moments to appreciate what was happening, express gratitude, and bless these situations. Rather than tune-in to release in these situations, I tuned-in to feel my emotions blossoming during these wonderful, happy experiences! I turned-on to connect with the loving space of my heart and together, my heart and I were content to fully embrace such magnificence. With an open heart, I reaffirmed my desire to continue to experience opportunities like these and share them with other people in my life.

I felt blessed to learn that I could tune-in to express gratitude for experiencing such happiness bouncing around me. Turning-on to connect with my heart enabled me to fully embrace the moment as it was and appreciate the many blessings that were arising in my life. I was now noticing the divinity of life around me and was extremely grateful to be part of many simple, blissful, happy experiences.

Requesting Guidance and Allowing

I was instinctively guided to apply *Time Out, Tune In, Turn On* to ask my heart for wise guidance on specific matters. On these occasions, I would take time out in a special place that was comfortable and quiet, usually in my garden or on my veranda. My tune-in process was to breathe in through my nose and out through my mouth, slowly and deeply, for as long as I needed. Then I would feel my feet root firmly into the earth, to ensure that I was grounded and present in the "here and now."

I would turn on and settle naturally into the sacred space of my heart, resting here, for a little while, experiencing peace. I would then spend a little time nourishing my relationship with my heart through loving acknowledgement. If I needed specific guidance, I would then ask and continue to rest whilst maintaining awareness and full acceptance that my answer would come.

Initially, I was pushy and searched for the surfacing of an answer, hoping it would instantaneously arrive. Over time, I developed patience and practised the process of allowing the answer to arrive in its own way and in its own time. On many occasions, I offered thanks to seal this process with my heart and then went on with my life in peace, even though I had received no answer. However, my answers did come eventually, on their own accord. I would then take another moment to tune in and reconnect with my heart, to contemplate the meaning of the wise guidance that I had received.

Whilst this was a gradual process of discovery, it was an incredibly beautiful opportunity to practise opening my heart, and providing space and time to allow my guidance to arrive. Through allowing, I practised patience and a more gentle way of life. I learnt to be kind on my loved ones, my life, and myself, and began to live more slowly, with grace and deep faith in the people and world around me. New opportunities were presenting and relationships were blossoming. Events in my life were synchronising and I was delighted with unexpected surprises.

Open Heart Connection

Recently, I spent some time in conversation with a new friend. We were sharing our honest realities and feelings. She then asked me for advice on a matter and went on to explain her concern in detail. We held each other in a space of stillness. I did not feel a need to jump in or put forth a proposal for her aid. I was comfortable listening from the space of my heart, which was open to caring, relating, and knowing. I was witnessing my new friend express a need to solve an issue of complexity.

With warm eyes and a kind smile, my arms gestured upward and outward, and I found myself saying with gentle reassurance, "There, you have it—you know what you need." She was perplexed and replied, "What do you mean?" My heart elaborated through my gentle voice, "You may not know your answer right now, but trust. Take some space, release, find your heart and ask. You answer may come right away and if not, give it time. You may be surprised when it arrives." There was understanding, compassion, and unity in our social connectivity.

In this process, I learnt that by turning-on, I opened my heart and offered a loving space to nurture our communication and interactive experience. When other people also open their heart, a heart connection is shared and unity in heart space is experienced.

Heart space is free of the need to judge and problem solve. It nurtures appreciation, allowing, and compassionate acceptance for what is, as it is, in-the-moment. Heart space enables people to experience their journey of life at their own pace, in their own way, along their unique path, whilst feeling connected, supported, and cared for socially.

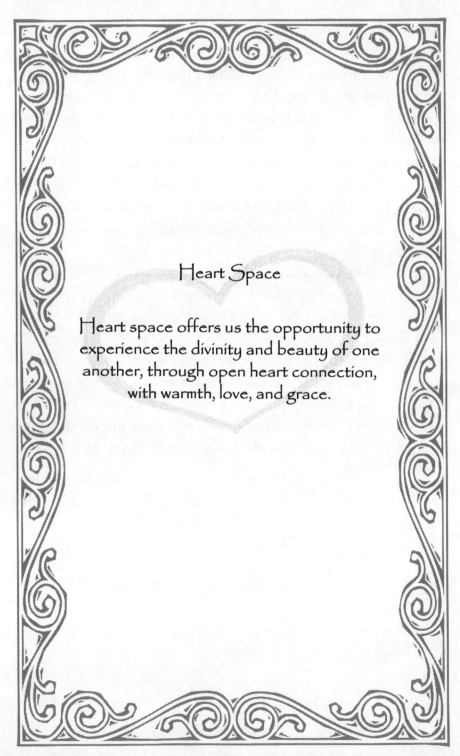

Heart Space

Heart space offers us the opportunity to
experience the divinity and beauty of one
another, through open heart connection,
with warmth, love, and grace.

Summary

After deeper reflection over time, I discovered that *Time Out, Tune In, Turn On* could be used in the heart of *any* moment. Initially, I applied *Time Out, Tune In, Turn On* in the heart of heated moments to survive and I recommend that you do so too. As your everyday life begins to change and you notice *Time Out, Tune In, Turn On* flows naturally for you, begin to apply this strategy to experience:

Heightened Awareness and
Compassionate Acceptance

Gratitude and Blessing

Requesting Guidance and Allowing

Open Heart Connection

Time Out, Tune In, Turn On is a strategy that will support you to embrace many elements of life change:

Release old habits and pain.

Honour your good feelings.

Source your true desires.

Receive inner guidance.

Open your heart.

Share graceful social connections.

Develop healthy boundaries.

Embrace beauty and spontaneity.

Be kind on yourself and other people.

Develop faith in your self-guided abilities.

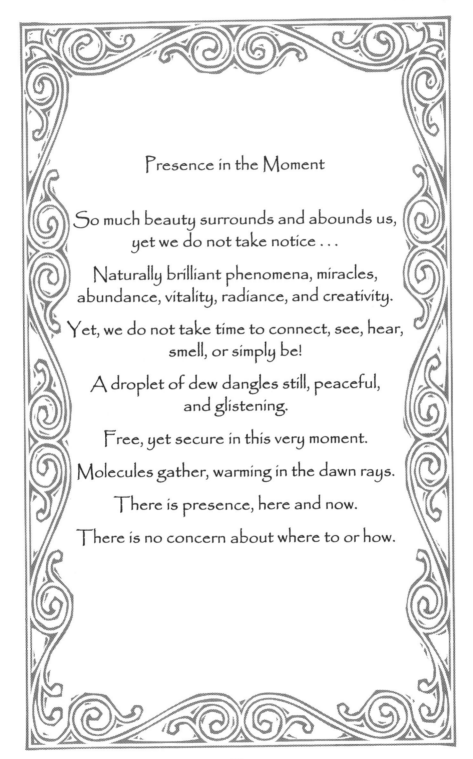

Presence in the Moment

So much beauty surrounds and abounds us,
yet we do not take notice . . .

Naturally brilliant phenomena, miracles,
abundance, vitality, radiance, and creativity.

Yet, we do not take time to connect, see, hear,
smell, or simply be!

A droplet of dew dangles still, peaceful,
and glistening.

Free, yet secure in this very moment.

Molecules gather, warming in the dawn rays.

There is presence, here and now.

There is no concern about where to or how.

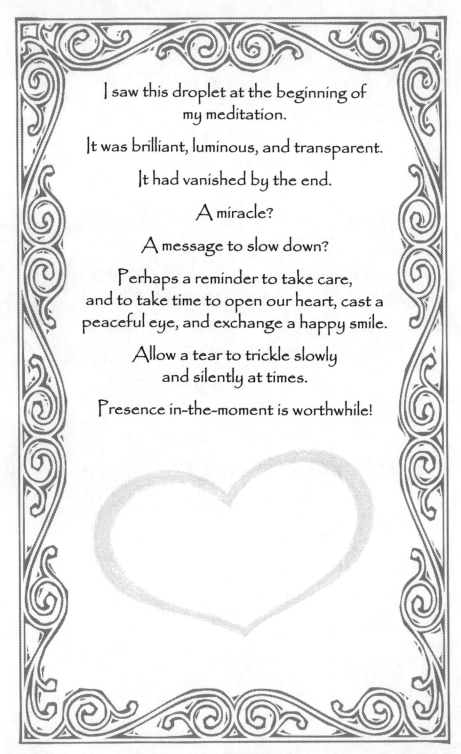

I saw this droplet at the beginning of
my meditation.

It was brilliant, luminous, and transparent.

It had vanished by the end.

A miracle?

A message to slow down?

Perhaps a reminder to take care,
and to take time to open our heart, cast a
peaceful eye, and exchange a happy smile.

Allow a tear to trickle slowly
and silently at times.

Presence in-the-moment is worthwhile!

Chapter 9

Embracing Change

On the day I decided to make a change in my life, I was not consciously aware that I actually *desired* life change. In fact, I was surprised that I had the courage to take the first step in a direction of something new. Perhaps my courage was a dormant quality, tucked away in the closet behind the coats of tight composure that had come to fit me so well.

I did not have a conscious realisation and I had not made any affirmation that I was going to take a step in a new direction, let alone embark on a journey of life change. However, I must have had a desire for a different life experience on a deeper level, for I was becoming increasingly dissatisfied with the challenges that I was coming up against, time after time. I knew deep down that my life could be different—I wanted a lighter, vibrant, and flowing life. Deep down, my heart desired change and I desired change too.

If I consciously knew that sitting down at the table was going to lead me in the direction of life change, I really do not think I would have been brave enough to follow through and complete such a shift—the concept of *life change*, is in all honesty, daunting to me. My mind feasts on platters filled with concern and worry . . . What will happen? How will I do it? Where will I start? What will this mean? The concept of "life change" was too hard for me to digest—I could not get it past my head, let alone see how it felt in my chest!

Perhaps that was why I was becoming so encumbered and confronted with reams of situations, filled with challenges to push through or try to resist. The path of resistance was hard work and I was brought up to work hard. On some level, I had a belief that *this must be my fair load*. I was squashing my heart and bursting the seeds of joy in my life. I was shutting down and closing off. I even stopped dreaming about what a different life would be like, for I was so focussed on working hard, diligently sorting my way through the testing times with my head down and back to the light.

Deep down, I wanted a break, I needed a break and I wished someone would give me a break or at the very least, "cut me some slack." I did not realise at the time that only I could cut myself free.

On the day I turned my back on the heated situation and left to sit down at the table to write, I unplugged from the hard-stuff and set myself free. I took time out with my cold coffee and instantly experienced a new reality. I did not realise exactly what was happening and I was not concerned about the details. However, after walking out the door that day, I knew that I was going to turn my back on the "hard stuff" and walk away whenever I felt zipped up tight.

I did not do this consistently, but I did it often enough to begin to thrive on a series of delightful, new experiences that I was now creating in my life. It was a small, yet significant step, to achieve much needed relief—to cool-off in the heart of a heated situation and revive. This quick, easy fix became my new addiction—I began to seek relief through writing regularly!

When I closed the door and meandered up the garden path, I set a new intention. It was not for life change—it was much simpler than that! It was to *do one thing new*—to leave unhealthy situations to sit, write, and experience relief. I did not know at the time, that I was using *Time Out, Tune In, Turn On* as a survival strategy, or that I would gradually experience results in the direction of life change.

Whilst I introduce *Time Out, Tune In, Turn On* to you and highlight how this strategy can support you to create change in your everyday life, I feel it is best to leave my intricate experiential stories for you to digest at your own pace in the "Heart-of-the-Moment Learning Resource." Right now, I would to suggest that you conduct the following experiment before putting *Time Out, Tune In, Turn On* to the test.

Creating Change in a Fun and Easy Way

This experiment will guide you to stay grounded and focussed on the here and now—on the life that is in front of you, to determine your readiness for change:

1. **Set a new intention:** Decide to do *one thing new*. Keep your intention simple—a one-off, new thing that you can do for yourself. This could be something that becomes a regular part of your life after this experiment, if you choose. For example, lighting a candle for your evening meal or turning the radio off for a little while when you drive.

2. **Action your intention:** Take the step to commit with action and follow through on your intention. Do the one thing that you have decided to do.

3. **Review:** Were you able to set a new intention and complete the action? How did this feel?

Repeat this experiment as often as you desire. You may choose to set another intention, or maybe two, three, or four!

This experiment will enable you to determine your level of readiness for change in a fun, easy, natural, and practical way. If you discover that you are able to action a new intention, be sure to celebrate your success, for you have overcome the hurdle of *resistance to change*.

Experiencing change in a fun and easy way has a number of benefits:

Self-Responsibility: Only you can decide when you are ready to try something new. Take a step in a new direction and action a new intention.

Inner Courage: Your ability to action a new intention rests deep within you. A single new action will create a shift, but will your inner courage surface to support you to persist?

Self-Confidence: Knowing that you can create a new intention and experience a positive outcome from your new action is rewarding and very fulfilling! We are our own catalysts for life change and we are capable of much more than we realise!

Self-Empowerment: You will be empowered to embrace life change as a journey, and to open-up to the joy of learning, healing, and growing, at your own pace, with your unique style.

Life Change

Life change is amazing and it really can just happen. There is nothing big or dramatic that you need to do. It is more about the process you go through. Whenever possible, take time out to tune in and turn on while you enjoy the ride! Laughing was a sign that I was living light, centred in my heart, juggling bubbles of wonderful opportunities as they popped into and out of my life, with each event and person offering a unique and ever-changing experience.

Intention and Action

Once you are changing freely and are comfortable with the concept of *life change*, you may wish to apply *Time Out, Tune In, Turn On* to experiment with change in your everyday life.

Time Out, Tune In, Turn On is a strategy with the three steps defined however, you are your own guide. You determine when you take time out and where you go. You do as you need to release with the materials you have at the time. You determine how long you need to rest in the scared space of your heart. Only you decipher the arising of your desires and the feeling of knowing when you receive wise guidance.

When practicing *Time Out, Tune In, Turn On* each step requires that you be guided by your *intention*—your own sense of what you know you need to do, and *action*—what you actually choose to do.

Intention

If you would like to experience the effects of applying *Time Out, Tune In, Turn On* in your everyday life, you will benefit from setting three new intentions. For example:

1. **Time Out:** I intend to leave a heated situation.

2. **Tune In:** I intend to release what I need to privately, with what I have, in a way that is natural for me.

3. **Turn On:** I intend to rest in the sacred space of my heart and open-up to what this experience offers.

In a self-guided reality, you are always free to modify your intentions and create new intentions as your journey unfolds. Once you have set your intentions and given yourself time to refine them, you are ready to take action.

Action

I needed time to develop and strengthen my inner courage and confidence in my ability to take action to create life change. I am glad I was kind on myself. Small steps were enough to create new everyday life experiences. By writing and reflecting on what I had written, I was able to appreciate the small steps that I was taking. They were very significant, yet they were easily overlooked amidst the busy pace of my full life.

When you apply *Time Out, Tune In, Turn On*, you will need to take three new actions:

1. **Time Out:** Leave a heated situation and find a quiet, private space. When you take time out, you will need to follow through and leave the situation. Try not to engage the mind—just know that you will spontaneously action this step when the time is ripe for you.

> The first time I took time out in the heart of a
> heated moment was my first step complete.
> The rest took care of itself!

2. **Tune In:** Release as you need to, with the materials you have access to at the time. Once you have taken time out, releasing will be easy because you will have your own private space and time. Try not to engage the mind—do what flows naturally for you.

3. **Turn On:** Rest in the sacred space of your heart and place your attention there. Observe how you feel and then observe the arising of your heart's desires and wise guidance.

It is easy to overlook the process of turning-on after you have taken time out to tune in because you will already feel so much better. Committing to action the third step will ensure you connect with your heart and complete your *Time Out, Tune In, Turn On* experience. Developing a new, sensitive relationship with your precious heart takes time and patience.

Taking the first step in using a new strategy can be daunting. If you feel uneasy or uncertain, please take care to be patient with yourself. You may need to experience making a change in the form of a visualisation as a process of preparation. This will enable you to develop your courage and confidence in creating life change, at a time and in an environment that suits you.

Writing about your experience and reflecting on your writing is an invaluable method to observe your progress and deepen your process of learning, healing, and personal growth. Write about how you feel, set it aside, and return to read your writing another time. Trust that you are developing knowledge now and that your application of *Time Out, Tune In, Turn On* will begin when you are ready—by its very nature of being self-guided strategy.

The "Heart-of-the-Moment Learning Resource" will guide your application of *Time Out, Tune In, Turn On* in a gentle, progressive way—you will always be the one who determines when, where, what, and how. In being your own guide, you have the opportunity to experiment with the versatility of this strategy, as it suits you, in your everyday life.

If you are ready to embrace a journey of life change using *Time Out, Tune In, Turn On*, you are ready to explore the "Heart-of-the-Moment Learning Resource."

Summary

I had an intention to change and acted on my intention without realising what I was doing on a conscious level. I did something different and it worked—I'm lucky I recorded my experience, for when I reviewed my writing, I realised that my first step triggered a series of new actions which resulted in "life change."

Repetition of a single, simple, new pattern fertilised my desire to continue to create delightful, new experiences. I also created a new belief—I *was* able to live in the direction of my true desires, in alignment with the path of my heart. My inner courage to remove myself from unhealthy situations increased in strength. I developed confidence in my ability to embrace change and create fulfilling, new experiences. I developed awareness that my experiences in life could change for the better, and that it was my responsibility to determine when, where, and how this would take effect. I felt empowered.

Reflection on my journal entries was an enlightening process. I discovered that I embarked on a journey of living the path of my heart which created changes in my personality, relationships, decision-making, and environment.

By embracing change, I was empowered to:

- Use my inner courage to cut myself free from my old perceptions and habitual responses in challenging situations.

- Give myself time and space to express my thoughts, feelings, and emotional reality.

- Confront my pain and the hold it had on me.

- Gradually experience a new way of being and gently nurture new feelings into my life.

- Reignite and nourish a loving relationship with my heart.

- Trust that the rising of desires and wise guidance from my heart would illuminate my way, along the path of my heart.

- Be kind and gentle on myself, and with other people.

- Have faith that small steps lead to profound results.

- Allow my self-guided process of life change to unfold naturally and gracefully, in its own time, and in a way that was unique to me.

Lovingly acknowledge what I really needed.

Take responsibility for my life experiences and remain confident in my ability to cope with change.

My journey of life change showed me how to *live*. As an adult, I am grateful that I did not rely on anybody, to address my needs or solve my problems, for this was my own responsibility.

I allowed my life change to be a gradual, self-guided process. I took small steps and was patient with myself. I did not have a grand goal or push to achieve a particular outcome. I simply decided to remove myself from heated situations whenever I needed to, and write to experience relief. There were occasions when I did not write and I released using my body. If I had access to other materials and felt compelled to use them, I did so. It was lovely to feel free from the unhealthy situation that would have previously consumed me. I was resting more frequently in the space of my heart and I was gaining reassurance that this was the direction for me.

Resources are invaluable guides to us. We all have unique, individual needs that change all the time. If you come across a resource or are attracted to a resource at a particular point in time, it is usually right for you. However, I wonder, have we lost touch with our own *inner resource*, our instinctual, self-guided ability to learn, heal, and grow naturally?

Time Out, Tune In, Turn On is a strategy that will support you on an amazing journey of life change. By applying *Time Out, Tune In, Turn On* you will renew your being, reshape your life, and live the path of your heart!

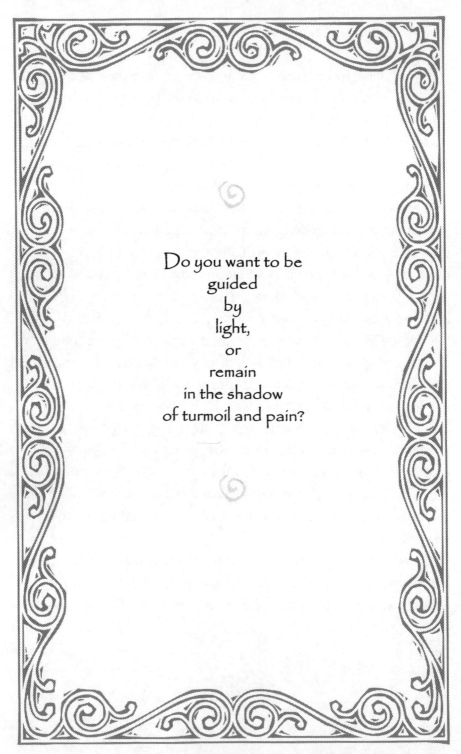

Do you want to be
guided
by
light,
or
remain
in the shadow
of turmoil and pain?

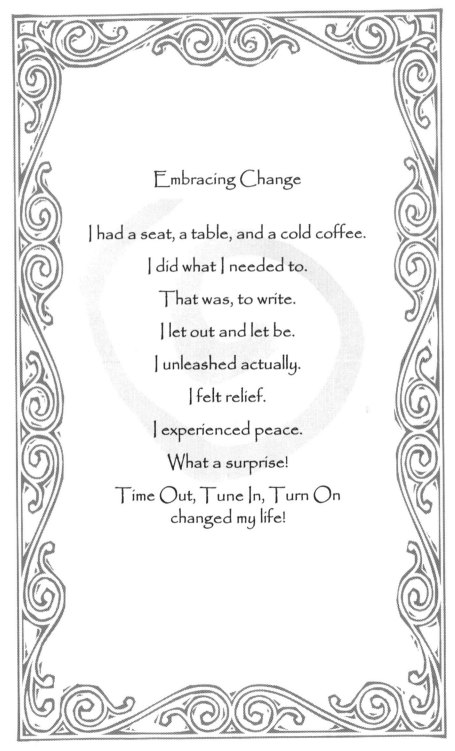

Embracing Change

I had a seat, a table, and a cold coffee.

I did what I needed to.

That was, to write.

I let out and let be.

I unleashed actually.

I felt relief.

I experienced peace.

What a surprise!

Time Out, Tune In, Turn On
changed my life!

Heart-of-the-Moment
Learning Resource

Chapter 10

Introduction

Time Out, Tune In, Turn On emerged as a self-discovered survival strategy and evolved into a self-guided strategy for living the path of your heart in everyday life.

By reflecting on my journal entries and revealing my learning, healing, and growth, I felt assurance from my heart that my story of discovery and experience in applying *Time Out, Tune In, Turn On* would engage and inspire my audience. I was tempted to share my story of life change by compiling my journal entries and reflections into a book, but I was not completely at peace with this vision in my heart. I needed to give this issue room to breathe and knew that my answer would emerge in its own time, from the wise sanctuary of my heart.

I was instinctively guided to apply *Time Out, Tune In, Turn On* a number of times whilst I cradled my beautiful, soft-violet, carved amethyst heart. I turned-on to connect with my heart and nurtured my new loving intention. I asked my heart, "How can I reach out and help people in such trying times?" I wanted to help people shed pain, embrace self-guided life change, and balance their duties with their hearts' desires. I wanted to contribute to the evolution of humanity, as an advocate for living the path of the heart.

I rested many times in the sacred space of my heart and allowed my answer to arise through the harmonious resonance of peace. With loving welcome, my answer eventually came as: "Engage, inspire, teach." As with most of my inner guidance, I needed to reconnect with my heart again, to fully understand and appreciate the meaning and application of the guidance I received.

I was grateful to receive verification that my journal entries and story of life change would engage and inspire my audience. But now, I received guidance to *teach*.

Teaching sounded logical but it took me some time to reach smooth acceptance and understanding of what this would involve: I was to teach how to apply *Time Out, Tune In, Turn On* if I were using this strategy for the first time.

My task, as guided from my heart, was to share my story of life change and my real-life experiences, in addition to developing a learning resource to support and guide readers in how to apply *Time Out, Tune In, Turn On* in everyday life. The learning resource would offer readers the opportunity to experiment with the versatility of this strategy, record their experiences, and then return at another time to reflect upon their learning, healing, and growth as it naturally occurs along their journey of life change. Therefore, I decided to develop an interactive resource which is based on learning from real-life experiences in the *heart-of-the-moment*. This would offer readers a complete learning experience, using practical, everyday exercises, which can be applied with flexibility, in the reader's own time.

I have therefore developed the "Heart-of-the-Moment Learning Resource" to offer readers:

- Guidance and support.

- Flexibility and choice.

- Preparation and practise.

- Versatility in application and experience.

- Recording and reflection.

Chapter 11

Reader's Guide

M y wish is to do more than share the *Time Out, Tune In, Turn On* strategy with you and then leave it to you, to put to the test. Of course, this is what you can do, if it suits you.

We all have different learning styles. Some readers may choose to apply *Time Out, Tune In, Turn On* straight away, naturally, in their own self-guided way. Other readers may need more time to digest, contemplate, prepare, and practise at a time that is convenient and in an environment that is quiet and comfortable. They may require additional guidance and support to make a start, and may also benefit from the focus of a theme, especially if life change is a new concept.

I have therefore developed the "Heart-of-the-Moment Learning Resource" to accompany your own, self-guided approach in applying *Time Out, Tune In, Turn On* in everyday life. You will be presented with a range of opportunities to explore the versatility of this strategy. You will have the benefit of choosing where, when, and how you begin to apply it. The exercises in this resource will also offer you flexibility in determining which elements of your life you would like to change.

In chapters two to six, you will have developed an understanding of how *Time Out, Tune In, Turn On* was discovered, and how it evolved as a strategy for everyday life change. In chapters seven and eight, you will have gained insight into the self-guided nature and versatile application of this strategy. In chapter nine, you will have begun to experiment with intention and action as important elements for creating change.

After the "Introduction" and "Reader's Guide" in chapters ten and eleven respectively, the "Heart-of-the-Moment Learning Resource" presents a series of eight chapters, from chapter twelve to nineteen. Each chapter in this resource offers a complete learning experience in relation to a particular theme and is presented in two parts:

Part I
Everyday Experience

Part II
Reader's Journal

The information that follows provides an outline for how each chapter is structured and offers suggestions for how the exercises may be used.

Part I: Everyday Experience

Each chapter begins with an everyday experience which I would like to share with you because it provides an example of how I applied *Time Out, Tune In, Turn On* in the heart-of-the-moment, during an everyday life situation. I also write about my insights which were revealed when I returned at a later stage to reflect on my journey.

1. **Journal:** My journal entry is raw, frank, honest, and real. It serves as a story for you to enjoy. On a deeper level, I invite you to witness the inner workings of my life—my humble reality as mother and wife.

2. **Reflection:** I have written my reflection after a period of personal growth. I have come back at a later stage to review my experience and reflect on my learning, healing, and personal growth. I have also used my reflection as an opportunity to explain how I applied *Time Out, Tune In, Turn On* in the situation which is described in my journal entry. Learning, healing, and growth is a process of inner alchemy, and in each reflection, I have shared my understanding of this

process. I have presented four quotes after each reflection to summarize the "theme" of my everyday life change experience. As a result, each chapter presents a new theme. Each theme will resonate with a different level of intensity in relation to your life experiences.

Reflection was the process which enabled me to discover *Time Out, Tune In, Turn On*. By reflecting on my journal entries, I realised that *Time Out, Tune In, Turn On* was a self-guided strategy with versatile application for creating everyday life change. I was able to observe my progress and see that I was making improved decisions from a centred, peaceful space. I was reassured that my life was changing and that my simple, small steps were effective. I discovered what was true and important to my heart, and received the guidance I needed at the time. I was able to witness my journey of learning, healing, and personal growth.

Part II: Reader's Journal

Each of the eight chapters in the learning resource also contain a "Reader's Journal" which provides an opportunity for you to participate in a range of exercises to support your application of *Time Out, Tune In, Turn On*.

As *Time Out, Tune In, Turn On* is a self-guided strategy, it is up to you to determine which exercises you would like to complete. Some people may feel ready to apply *Time Out, Tune In, Turn On* in everyday situations straight away, as they naturally arise. Other people may require a more progressive approach, over a longer period of time. In this case, applying *Time Out, Tune In, Turn On* using visualisation will be a supportive and effective exercise.

The journal has space for you to record your experiences and reflections. You may choose to record your writing in the space provided or create a system of your own. I encourage you to keep a record of your experiences and reflections, so that over time, you may:

Discover your true feelings.

Reveal, confront, and release your patterns of pain.

Receive and appreciate the loving wisdom
that arises from your heart.

Witness your seeds of desire sprout in
alignment with the path of your heart.

Demystify the concept of "connecting with your
inner light" and "living from your heart."

Develop awareness of "synchronicity."

Reveal dormant personal qualities.

Develop reassurance that you are navigating the
direction of your life with integrity and sensitivity.

Develop compassion for yourself, other
people, and a life-long healing journey.

In time, you may be ready to share your writing—the workings of your inner world. It is important to celebrate your journey of life change and it is for you to decide, when and how to share your story.

Time Out, Tune In, Turn On Using Visualisation

1. **Recall:** You are invited to recall a recent, challenging event in your life and attend to what happened, what you did, and how you felt. In the early chapters, this exercise will awaken you to patterns of control, reactivity, suppression, and submission. In the latter chapters, this exercise will awaken you to opportunities for expressing gratitude and embracing spontaneity, creativity, and synchronicity. In each chapter, you may awaken a desire to set a new intention for change in relation to this situation or the chapter theme.

2. **Visualisation:** This technique will prepare you to take the first steps along your path of life change, particularly if you feel that it would be easier to put off or try some other time. Visualisation will clear your path from mental blocks, negative mind-sets, and beliefs. You will build confidence in your ability to set a new intention and see yourself in action, in alignment with this desire.

   You are invited to visualise yourself in a recent situation and see yourself recreating your reality through application of *Time Out, Tune In, Turn On*. For many people, visualisation may be a new experience. You will strengthen your intention to change and develop confidence in your ability to embrace change through the process of visualisation. For some people, visualisation will be an important part of your preparation. Visualisation will enable you to experience shifts and create change in your everyday life at a time and in a place that is convenient and comfortable.

Setting aside some time in a quiet, private space to complete your visualisation exercise will enable you to apply *Time Out, Tune In, Turn On* without anxiety, pressure, distractions, or interruptions.

I have written a series of steps to guide you through the process of visualisation using *Time Out, Tune In, Turn On*. When learning visualisation, it is normal to first read a step, then close your eyes while you complete the step, and then open your eyes to read the next step. Do not try to memorise every step from the outset. As you practise this technique, you will develop familiarity and will naturally proceed through each step with your eyes closed.

This is an example of how the visualisation section is structured in each chapter:

Time Out*:* See yourself taking solo space. Is there anything you say? Where do you go?

Tune In*:* See yourself letting out and letting go. Release your thoughts and feelings. How does it feel to release all that you need to, honestly and completely? Do you see yourself calm and peaceful? Do you feel a change in your physical being?

Turn On: Stay a little longer to rest with your feeling of calm and peace. Rest in the safe space of your heart. Look around, what do you see? Is there anything you wish to ask? Do not be discouraged if you do not see light, feel your desires, or sense the emerging of wise guidance. You will naturally experience the arising of new desires and the flow of wise guidance if it is relevant for you in this moment. (This may sound very new to you, perhaps too new, but I encourage you to take a step and try it. Then you will know about this experience from doing.)

At this stage, you may choose to follow the additional prompts that relate to the chapter theme. It is important to give yourself time in this safe, peaceful heart space and trust that all you need to know will arise, if it is what you need at the time.

When you feel you have spent enough time in your heart space and know you are ready to complete your turn-on process, offer thanks and go on with your life in peace.

By applying *Time Out, Tune In, Turn On* using visualisation, you may be surprised with how easy it is to do. You may experience immediate changes in your physical being and in what you go on to do in your life. If you apply *Time Out, Tune In, Turn On* using visualisation and find it to be a challenging experience, you may find that your challenges subside as you practise this exercise over time. If challenges continue to persist, this may not be your time.

Applying *Time Out, Tune In, Turn On* using visualisation may create immediate changes in how you feel and in your outlook on life. You can practise the visualisation exercise as frequently and as regularly as you desire. This exercise will ignite your inspiration to use *Time Out, Tune In, Turn On* in an everyday situation when the time is ripe for you. Visualisation will nurture your self-confidence and ability to embrace everyday life change using a sensitive, graceful, and progressive approach.

3. **Record:** Upon completion of your visualisation using *Time Out, Tune In, Turn On*, you are invited to write about your experience in as much detail as possible. Writing about your experiences, unfiltered thoughts, and feelings is a healing process and provides a record for you to reflect upon at a later stage. Usually, a crisis or significant life event cracks us open to allow the light in and provide an opportunity to learn, heal, and grow. Writing is a simple, private way to allow energy to flow. Instead of putting-off or holding-in, we can use writing to let out and let go, experience relief, and simultaneously learn, heal, and grow. You will also have a record to look back upon someday.

4. **Reflect:** Returning at a later stage to review your experience and reflect on your learning, healing, and growth will gradually reveal your personal journey of life change. Reflection is a process of reading your writing and attending to the gist of what is going on. It provides an opportunity to discover the deeper meaning of what you are experiencing in life. Since you are reading from a different point in time, you have a fresh perspective and are clear of emotional cobwebs that can smother you, when the pressure is on. Through reflection, you will get to know your inner world and discover who you are becoming at different times in your life.

Reflection also provides much needed support and acknowledgement when you realise that you are making changes and experiencing growth in the direction of your heart's desire. Reflection strengthens your will and determination to develop transparency in all aspects of your life. You will experience clarity in your decision-making and shape your destiny with integrity.

The Power of Reflection

We can learn so much from the events that are happening around us and within us. In our busy, full lives, there is often so much happening that we don't make time to reflect on our experiences, let alone plunge into the depths of dissatisfaction and stagnation. Reflection reveals patterns in our life experiences during day-to-day events—patterns that occur around us, and inside our body, heart, and mind. These patterns direct the course of our lives. So, if we do not check in, how do we know where are we going?

Learning to Live

When we learn from life and allow ourselves to heal, we become whole and sprout new growth. We create new experiences to refine our desires. We accept our responsibility and our unique ability to be the artist of the life we create. Take time out and tune in. What is going on in your life? How do you feel? What does this information reveal? Turn on. What do you desire? What does your heart guide you to do?

Time Out, Tune In, Turn On in Everyday Life

You will know when you are ready to apply *Time Out, Tune In, Turn On* in an everyday life situation. We all have different learning styles. Some people will be able to apply *Time Out, Tune In, Turn On* in everyday life without needing to prepare through visualisation. Other people may need to take more time to prepare.

When you begin to apply *Time Out, Tune In, Turn On*, consider applying this strategy in a familiar environment, so that you know where you can go to take time out. Also consider informing the relevant people in your life, so they will be aware that you are exploring the effectiveness of a new strategy. Rest assured that you will naturally use this strategy when you need to. That way, you will use *Time Out, Tune In, Turn On* when you are ready, without over-thinking or over-trying. This could happen immediately if you have been inviting change into your life.

Time Out, Tune In, Turn On is a strategy with three simple steps and they will unfold naturally, if you have set an intention to create change and then take action. You need no further guiding steps to apply *Time Out, Tune In, Turn On* in everyday life situations. Simply be guided by how you feel.

When you tune in, it is important that you release as you feel you need to, with the materials you have access to at the time. You may not always use writing to tune in. Ensure you give yourself enough time to rest in the safe, peaceful space of your heart when you turn on. It is likely that you will feel better immediately after tuning-in, and if you choose to move on with your life after tuning-in, without turning-on, you will move away from the precious opportunity to connect with your loving heart.

5. **Record:** You are invited to record your experience in applying *Time Out, Tune In, Turn On* in everyday situations, either at the time you apply the strategy, or at another time that suits you—when it happens naturally for you. Whilst recording your experience will provide an opportunity for reflection at another time, do not push yourself to record every experience.

   If you choose to write to release and record your experiences frequently, you will naturally develop a method to accommodate your preferences and patterns. You may write to release as a form of tuning-in. You may write about your experiences in using *Time Out, Tune In, Turn On* after you give thanks and move on with your life in peace. You may write at another time in the day. If you have the desire to write, use whatever you have with you, even if it is a quick note on a piece of scrap paper. You can then stick the note into this journal or another personal journal at a time that suits you.

6. **Reflect:** You are also invited to reflect on your experience of applying *Time Out, Tune In, Turn On* during everyday situations when you feel drawn to do so. You may also give consideration to the prompts that relate to the chapter theme. Reflection will reveal your story of learning, healing, and growth. You may make notes or just "take note." You may realise different things about yourself—there may be some things that you like and there may be some things that ignite a new desire for change. You may surprise yourself with how quickly you are evolving.

   Some of the prompts will guide you to consider: Is your life changing and if so, how? Are you learning anything about yourself? Have any desires or beads of wise guidance emerged from your heart? How are people responding to you?

Reviewing your writing will culture insight and you will discover your becoming. Enjoy this process and when you are ready, share your writing and findings with someone. This is an important process of honouring and celebrating your journey of life change.

Summary

The self-guided exercises in the "Heart-of-the-Moment Learning Resource" are repeated in each chapter to offer a framework of support for you to apply *Time Out, Tune In, Turn On* and record your experiences and reflections over time.

By completing the exercises in each chapter, you will be well and truly under way with giving *Time Out, Tune In, Turn On* a "go." You will have had a range of opportunities to experience and evaluate the effectiveness of this strategy in creating change in your life. Even if your changes are slight, there will be no self-doubt, as you will have a written record of your progress. If you do not feel drawn to participate in the exercises or if you experience any on-going difficulty, this may be a sign that now it is not your time and that is okay.

Whilst the exercises in the learning resource may be beneficial and important to your personal growth and life change, it is equally important to engage in some form of creative activity in your life every day. Creativity facilitates energetic flow—change is movement of energy. The mind lets go, blocks break free, and fresh energy flows. Immerse yourself in an activity you love such as jamming, composing, designing, building, sewing, crafting, decorating, gardening, cooking, painting, drawing, or colouring. Creativity is another process that is fuelled by "inner alchemy." Participation in creative activities will ensure that your gateway opens to facilitate personal growth and life change.

Begin to read and enjoy. The flow of the chapters will guide you through my most significant life-changing situations. These are times when my seed cracked and I was able to open to receive new light.

Chapter 12

'Bean' in
the Moment

Everyday Experience I

1. Journal

I never thought it would have an adverse consequence. Well, at the time, that is. You see, I did think it through, and I hedged my bets that he wouldn't really like it, and out it would come—slimy, maybe even bitten through, for it was certainly of adult taste and adult desire.

I already had mine. A surprise it was, to appear in slinky dark tones against the porcelain glow of my flat white. I was quick to notice the second and snatch it away with a brisk pinch, but silly me—I thought that I would go unnoticed.

Well, he didn't actually see me take it, as he was deeply engrossed in removing the dark-chocolate button on his mini mud cup cake. What gave it away was my expression, or perhaps my afterglow. You know—the look a woman gets upon complete, climactic satisfaction! Or, put more eloquently, the pregnant glow: shining eyes, squishy complexion, and a beaming smile, all supported by undeniable inner warmth.

That same warmth melted away every molecule of that tiny morsel of chocolaty caffeine. Dark chocolate it was, and of superb quality. It was a delightful little treat that I thought I had all to myself! But, just as I dared to take the second, he was searching for "it." Name, he didn't know, but he knew it was good. How right he was! How reluctant I was, to give it up; to see it go away to another beckoning body.

So, to soften my inner pain and deep attachment to a truly satisfying moment, enhanced by flavour and textural sensation, I tried to resist at last minute. I pleaded and reasoned: "Oh, please. It's not what you'd like! You've had your big chocolate button; this little one is mine!" Yet he insisted in the most dramatic manner, and I was instantly overcome—some fleeting weakness between mother and son! After all, we were in public.

I thought: He's only three. We sure do enjoy our velvet hot chocolates and soft, warm, baked buttery goods—it's important that we have a nice time. So I let him have it, thinking I might get it back. Mind sent a further rationalisation: Besides, it won't really have an effect!

Well, pay I did—for two nights through! He was buzzing and bouncing, far too wired to do anything focused or calm, let alone rest. Sleep wasn't in the equation, and irritability was my test.

This interesting journey was perhaps a lesson to stand strong. Or, perhaps a lesson to simply know better and admit I did wrong? Well, "wrong" is not quite the right word. I really tried to do my best!

I'll settle with putting it in the basket of learning and let you decide the rest!

2. Reflection

I struggled in standing firm and saying "no" to my little one, for fear of emotional escalation and a battle of wills in public. I surrendered my desire for that second coffee bean and talked myself into doing it. Little did I realise that a short, strong outburst on his part at the time could have saved days of irritability and erratic behaviour. But, my fear of social judgement dominated on this occasion. This sneaky pattern of pain was weaving its way back into my life again!

I admit, I didn't take time out in this moment. I was focused on my blissful sensation and desire to have that second chocolate-coated coffee bean!

However, I practised Time Out, Tune In, Turn On with determination and discipline in the days that followed. This was my sanity and basic survival strategy. I knew that I was responsible for the effect the caffeine had on my son. I knew I had to work through the consequence, rather than resist, as nothing would make the chaos and irritability go away. I knew there was no other way, than to ride it out. The only relief I was going to get was the relief I created for myself. It was my choice how.

Time Out, Tune In, Turn On was my survival strategy. In the next two days at home, I frequently retreated to my bedroom, closed my eyes, and breathed. My release was simple and momentary as I knew my son would soon find me. When I could, I stood in front of my window and stretched my neck, yawned, rolled my shoulders, and stretched my spine. My physical release was quick and effective, I could feel my resistance letting go.

Sitting down on my blanket box signalled my readiness to turn-on and retreat to my sacred haven within. Here, I reminded myself, "I am okay. I am real. I give myself permission to flow and grow." I felt refreshed, centred, and empowered to go on with my life, knowing that I could retreat to my special place whenever I was in need.

Then, I would go on with my life in peace. I repeated this process throughout the day. I am so grateful that I gave Time Out, Tune In, Turn On a fair go. This survival strategy became a new healthy habit for me. To this day, I am still so surprised that I made it through such a challenging time!

This experience was a wonderful opportunity for my personal growth. It was my responsibility to deal with it and more importantly, I was responsible for choosing how. I am proud of having compassionately embraced my son and this situation, thanks to my frequent use of Time Out, Tune In, Turn On. I gave myself permission to deal with this situation differently and felt supported on my new journey.

I also developed confidence in my ability to cope during this challenging time. I was responsible for what I created and there was no way out, so I settled into acceptance, using Time Out, Tune In, Turn On. I was able to return refreshed and centred, and I was able to compassionately embrace the chaos of my child's life. This was a situation that had consumed him, as a result of his consuming that coffee bean!

It was nice for my husband to see me make it through and to know that he was sensing in me, a renewal of my coping ability. I was a sprouting seed. It was nice to show him that I could change my ways, the quality of my life during the day, and our quality of life in the evening as a family. I dare not even wonder what may have become of me without this survival strategy!

I also learnt to be kind to myself and not to strive to use Time Out, Tune In, Turn On all of the time, but to use it when it suited me. At the moment, that was at home and not yet publically.

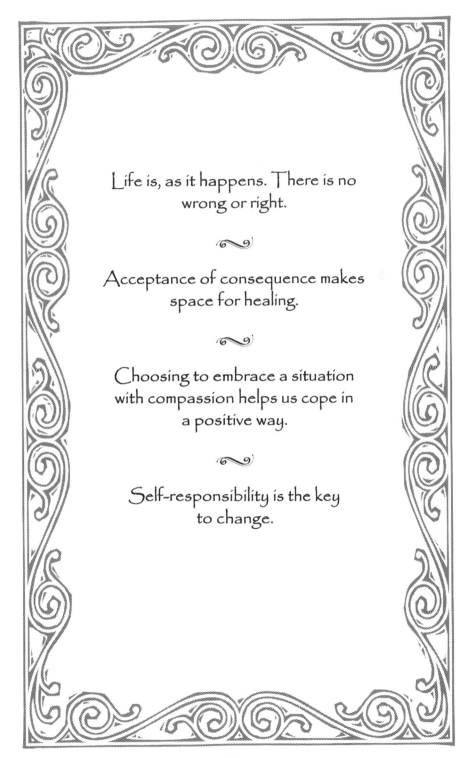

Life is, as it happens. There is no wrong or right.

Acceptance of consequence makes space for healing.

Choosing to embrace a situation with compassion helps us cope in a positive way.

Self-responsibility is the key to change.

Reader's Journal

Visualisation

1. **Recall:** Can you describe a recent situation where you had to work through a challenge that was inevitable?

....

....

....

....

....

....

....

....

....

....

....

....

....

....

2. **Visualise:** Close your eyes. See yourself in this situation. Imagine applying *Time Out, Tune In, Turn On* as your survival strategy:

Time Out: Find solo space.
Take a moment for yourself.
Breathe and simply be.

Tune In: Do as you need to release.
Let the process flow naturally for you.
Experience relief.

Turn On: Stay with your feeling of relief.
Connect within.
Rest in the safe space of your heart.
Feel centred and experience peace.
Trust that you can return to this place,
whenever you need.
When you are ready, offer thanks.
Go on with your life in peace.

3. **Record:** Write about your experience in applying *Time Out, Tune In, Turn On* as a survival strategy during visualisation with as much detail as possible:

   Time Out: What did you do? Where did you go?

   Tune In: How did you release? What did you have access to?

   Turn On: Were you able to experience peace? What did your heart reveal?

   ....

   ....

   ....

   ....

   ....

   ....

   ....

   ....

   ....

   ....

   ....

   ....

   ....

   ....

4. **Reflect:** Upon returning at a later stage and reviewing the notes you have made, what did your visualisation experience reveal?

Did you experience relief in your physical being after you released?

Do you feel more confident in applying *Time Out, Tune In, Turn On?*

Were you able to rest in the safe space of your heart?

What was it like to experience peace, soon after you removed yourself from a challenging situation?

....

....

....

....

....

....

....

....

....

....

....

....

Everyday Situation

5. **Record:** Were you able to apply *Time Out, Tune In, Turn On* in an everyday life situation today? A record of your experience is invaluable. Try to record your experience during each stage of *Time Out, Tune In, Turn On* with as much detail as possible:

Time Out: What did you do? Where did you go?

Tune In: How did you release? What did you have access to?

Turn On: Did you discover anything new?

....

....

....

....

....

....

....

....

....

....

....

....

....

....

6. **Reflect:** Upon returning at a later stage and reviewing the information you have recorded, what do you notice?

◎ Did *Time Out, Tune In, Turn On* help you survive a challenging situation?

◎ Have you experienced any difficulty using *Time Out, Tune In, Turn On*?

◎ Have you rediscovered your coping ability?

◎ Do you feel more confident in applying *Time Out, Tune In, Turn On* in everyday situations?

◎ Have people noticed a change in you?

....

....

....

....

....

....

....

....

....

....

....

Creations

Creations

Chapter 13

Breaking Free and Becoming

Everyday Experience II

1. Journal

I'm tired. It is winter, and he won't wear warm clothes. Internal heating doesn't quite make a difference to a sudden cold snap in a tiled, Queensland-style home with high ceilings and wide windows. I love these features for the summer though!

My beautiful boy now has a cold and is up all night. He is clingier than usual and still breastfeeding, at the age of three. This wears me down. I could say some affirmations to lift my spirit, but my heart is sad and my soul cries. Why are some things just so hard to do?

Flannelette pyjamas are normally warm and cosy, but mine are thin and worn. My feet are happy in woolly slippers and socks despite the clingy pill balls that gather between my toes. My bottom is cold from sitting on the lid of a toilet seat as I hide to cry again. This time it's in the en-suite—it has warmer tones. The sleeves on my arm are wet from soaking my tears and wiping my nose.

My beautiful boy soon finds me and says, "Mum, why are you upset?" I look up and say calmly, with a quiet air of despair, "Because you won't wear your warm clothes." His eyes were clear and bright and without hesitation, he says, "Mum, I still love you!" Then he gives me a cuddle. Caught by surprise I do something between laugh and cry. As we hold our embrace, I say, "I still love you too."

Before my next breath, he was up and away, and I was alone again. The toilet seat was now warm and comfortable and I recalled the details of the intense, yet fleeting event that bought me to this space. It was 4:34 a.m. I found his long-sleeve top and there was a chase ending in a tight little corner behind the couch. Screaming and yelling, you would think I'd hesitate, but I didn't want to give-in. My reasoning was logical and firm: it was winter, the heater was not on, and he already had a cold.

I did give in and I was so upset. I didn't know how to get through or how to get around the matter and decided to let it be. So here I sit, cried out, forgiven, and loved. I now know I'm okay. As I write, my tears dry and my nose breathes freely. I sigh as I begin to wonder: "Can I forgive myself?" A still, soft, warm sensation fills me. I close my eyes and rest with full appreciation. I see my inner light. I hear gentle reassurance, "Yes, forgiving yourself is easy." I feel at peace. Off to breakfast I go!

2. Reflection

It's not an easy road or a pleasant path for many of us at times. We experience challenges and complexities frequently, as a natural component of our lives. This experience has shown me that even the smallest challenge can teach us significant lessons.

I felt pathetic that I was hiding in my ensuite, crying in the early dawn hours because I couldn't dress my son with a manner of warmth, to achieve generation of warmth.

I released control and let my son experience the cold. In deciding to give up, I decided to take time out. I released control of the situation went to my ensuite to hide and cry. Time out in a private, secure space enabled me to tune-in and do what I needed to do. I freed my tears and they poured out. I didn't realise how much I needed to cry. My journal was in reach, so I started to write. I was so frustrated and upset that a simple task was such a challenge, so early in the morning!

I didn't ask to be forgiven. My son of three-years instinctively offered forgiveness! I naturally responded with forgiveness for him and our hearts united. Our challenging experience healed. He was up and away and I remained quiet and still, content to be alone in a loving, peaceful zone. This was a soothing experience and as I closed my eyes to settle into my heart, I turned-on.

I realised that I needed to lighten-up and not be so hard on myself. Upon accepting this, I realised that on a deeper level, I needed to forgive myself, and I needed to forgive myself frequently. I was reassured by the wise guidance of my heart that forgiving myself is easy and it was. My intention and connection in a loving heart space was all that I needed. I too, was then able to move on.

Applying Time Out, Tune In, Turn On in the heart of this heated situation reawakened me to the unconditional love that our children give, and deepened my understanding of the power of forgiveness. I also discovered a simple prerequisite—that in order to forgive one-another, we must first forgive ourselves.

As I reflect on this situation, I am deeply grateful for embracing everyday life change. I'm glad that I decided to give in, release control, and take time out to hide and cry. I'm glad that I tuned-in and honoured my need to cry, sob, and write. I'm glad that my son reached out to me, through a mist of unconditional love, just at the right moment, to offer loving forgiveness, without hesitation. I'm glad that we exchanged a complete, humble, healing embrace. I'm glad that my son moved on so quickly and that I gave myself more time to turn-on and rest in the peaceful, loving haven of my heart. I'm glad that I was guided to forgive myself in this moment and throughout my life frequently.

When I went on with my life and greeted my son, he greeted me with another surprise—he asked for his top to be put on. What a welcome a change!

It wasn't until I applied Time Out, Tune In, Turn On that I discovered I needed to forgive myself. I've known about the healing benefits of forgiveness and have embraced forgiving practice throughout my life. I know that forgiveness of one-another sets the foundation for healing, making peace, and moving forward. This experience opened my eyes to a new insight—to forgive one-another, we must first forgive ourselves.

Release of control creates room for healing.

To forgive another person, you must
first forgive yourself.

Mutual forgiveness ignites
relationship renewal.

Hearts heal with love and forgiveness.

Reader's Journal

Visualisation

1. **Recall:** Can you describe a recent situation where you have tried to achieve an outcome by pushing and imposing control?

....

....

....

....

....

....

....

....

....

....

....

....

....

....

....

....

2. **Visualise:** Close your eyes. See yourself in this situation. Imagine that you are recreating this scene whilst applying *Time Out, Tune In, Turn On:*

Time Out: Find solo space.
Take a moment for you.
Breathe and simply be.

Tune In: Do as you need to release.
Let the process flow naturally for you.
Experience relief.

Turn On: Connect within.
Rest in the safe space of your heart.
Feel at ease and experience peace.
What do you really desire?
Trust.
You will be guided to do as you need to,
at this time.
Do you need to forgive someone?
Do you need to forgive yourself?
When you feel ready, offer thanks.
Go on with your life in peace.

3. **Record:** Write about your experience in applying *Time Out, Tune In, Turn On* during visualisation with as much detail as possible:

Time Out: What did you do? Where did you go?

Tune In: How did you release? What did you have access to?

Turn On: Did you discover anything new?

....

....

....

....

....

....

....

....

....

....

....

....

....

....

....

....

4. **Reflect:** Upon returning at a later stage and reviewing the notes you have made, what did your visualisation experience reveal?

    Were you able to release control and create a new experience?

    Could you relax in your physical being?

    Did you experience peace?

    How did it feel to rest in the space of your heart?

    Is forgiving yourself a new concept to you?

    Has someone offered you forgiveness when you did not expect it?

....

....

....

....

....

....

....

....

....

....

Everyday Situation

5. **Record:** Were you able to apply *Time Out, Tune In, Turn On* in an everyday life situation today? A record of your experience is invaluable. Try to record your experience during each stage of *Time Out, Tune In, Turn On* with as much detail as possible:

Time Out: What did you do? Where did you go?

Tune In: How did you release? What did you use?

Turn On: Did you discover anything new?

....

....

....

....

....

....

....

....

....

....

....

....

....

6. **Reflect:** Upon returning at a later stage and reviewing the information you have recorded, what do you notice?

Are you becoming aware of habits or patterns of pain in your life?

Are emotions surfacing for expression and release?

Have any desires surfaced?

Have you received wise guidance?

Are you beginning to change your ways in everyday life?

....

....

....

....

....

....

....

....

....

....

....

....

Creations

Creations

Chapter 14

From Centre Stage to Background

Everyday Experience III

Ⅲ

1. Journal

I was brought up to work hard and reap the benefits, which were largely material wealth and social status. Now I am broke and have had no professional job for three-and-a-half years. How ironic!

Yet, I feel that I have changed more now than ever! Mainly in the way I sense and perceive the world. Naturally, there's been a change in the way people of the world perceive me—on a social scale, I am probably viewed as a lazy, over-attached mother on welfare who needs to put her child in care, get a job, and help my husband clear the debts.

I still don't know who I truly am, as I am changing so rapidly. Part of my habit of pain still seeks acknowledgement and gratitude from others for my efforts, loving, and giving. Being just "Mum" isn't that glamorous, and it's a job that doesn't come with benefits like flexible working hours, superannuation, annual leave, or sick days.

This is one of my greatest lessons at the moment—giving unconditionally and living with the depleted conditions that have resulted from my decisions. I am saddened. I'll get there. I know so.

Continue to give. Continue to love.

2. Reflection

I sat on my blanket box for time out. I started to write to tune-in. I needed to get this issue off my chest. It had been bugging me for a long while! My saga of discontent with doing something I love, yet finding life so hard at times, on top of doing it tough financially, was becoming a painful entity. It was something I needed to release.

I was relieved and so glad to vent this issue, even if I was my only audience at the time. If I didn't get this issue out, this saga would have hung around for another round later in the week! My pain was attached to dwelling in self-pity and this was beginning to bother me.

Tuning-in gave me the opportunity to experience and release my sadness, and acknowledge it as a real part of me. By feeling and writing, I let out. I no longer needed my sadness to cling to me so that I could continue to dwell in self-pity.

By turning-on, I was able to confront my pain within the safe space of my heart. I felt reassured that it was time to release my self-pity and accept my humble, yet harsh reality—fulfilling my desire to parent full-time was matched with a consequence of deleted financial and material conditions, despite the hard work, giving, and unconditional love that I was pouring into my family. This was an awkward, yet enlightening realisation for me to experience.

I was surprised that the wise guidance from my heart emerged so quickly and with such simplicity. I did not really understand my guidance at the time. In fact, I miss-understood it. In all honesty, I emerged from this experience feeling somewhat burdened. My message was to "continue to give and continue to love." Frankly, I was so tired of outpouring! This wasn't really the message I wanted to hear!

If I would have rested in the space of my mind, I would have moved into my life with lingering resentment. I am grateful for having taken the time to rest in the peaceful, loving haven of my heart. I experienced a deep knowing that I was okay and that it was necessary for me to continue to give and continue to love as I had been doing. I was able to cradle my knowing with loving acceptance and relax even more deeply. I was connected with my heart, and enjoyed the mutual nurturing experience we shared. I experienced a new feeling of being gentle with myself and with my heart. A delicate, sparkling inner alchemy was bubbling away inside as I experienced a new feeling of self-love.

Self-love was a concept I knew about, but had not yet experienced with this level of awareness. By spending extra time with my heart, I was able to understand the meaning of my wise message with new sensitivity.

My wise heart was guiding me to direct my efforts inward, not outward. Giving inwardly, was a new concept for me, especially in my role as a mother. I realise now that I have been caught in a cycle of outpouring. I had not considered that I needed to offer loving attention and care to myself and my heart. By realising that self-love is a basic necessity, I was now able to restore the balance of loving and giving in my life.

I felt a twinge of guilt and stupidity because it is quite logical that in order to love and give to others, we must be able to love and give to ourselves. I felt very blessed that I was able to forgive myself whilst I enveloped myself in tenderness and experienced mutual nourishment with my heart. This was a beautiful lesson and a much needed healing.

Now that I am aware, I can alter my pattern of habitual outpouring. I can make a change and direct loving attention and affection inward. As a regular ritual, I can take time out for myself, tune-in to release and turn-on to restore a healthy, loving relationship with my heart.

Self-love will now be my foundation for living with integrity. Judgements of other people and trends in society will no longer bother me, for I am now firmly grounded in what is important and true to me. Through self-love, I nourish my relationship with my heart, for my heart is my centre of support and together, we can restore balance in loving and giving, both inwardly and outwardly.

Through self-love, I experienced healing and awakening.

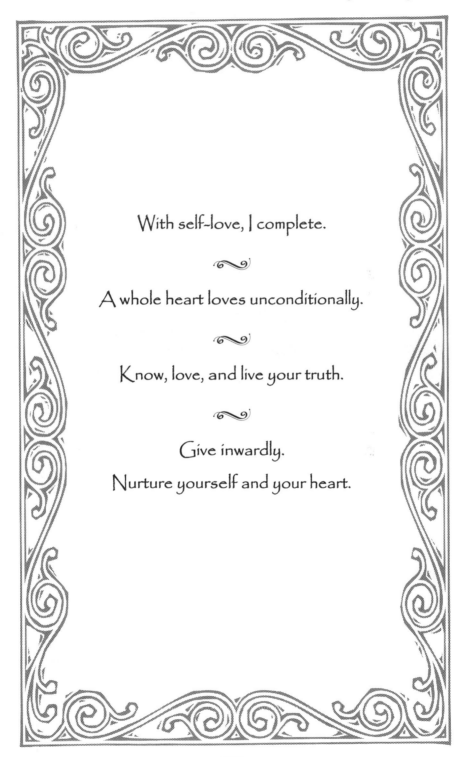

With self-love, I complete.

A whole heart loves unconditionally.

Know, love, and live your truth.

Give inwardly.
Nurture yourself and your heart.

Reader's Journal

Visualisation

1. **Recall:** Can you identify an issue that has been bothering you lately?

....

....

....

....

....

....

....

....

....

....

....

....

....

....

....

....

....

....

2. **Visualise:** Close your eyes. See yourself contemplating this issue. Now imagine yourself in a quiet, private, comfortable space. Take this opportunity to "get this issue off your chest" and open to receiving wise guidance from your heart. It may be natural for you to do this in real life, rather than using visualisation in this instance.

> **Time Out:** Find solo space. Take a moment for you. Breathe and simply be.
>
> **Tune In:** Release. Do what you need to do. Let the process of release flow naturally for you.
> In this instance, it would be beneficial to express all that you need to about this issue. State what it is and how you feel. Let yourself pour out.
>
> **Turn On:** Connect within. Feel at ease and experience peace.
> Rest and deepen your connection with your heart.
> Trust your wise guidance when it flows.
> Learn about yourself.
> Give yourself time to heal and grow.
> Your desires will arise, if they are relevant at this time.
> When you feel ready, offer thanks.
> Go on with your life in peace.

3. **Record:** Write about your experience in applying *Time Out, Tune In, Turn On* during visualisation, when you were contemplating the issue that was bothering you, with as much detail as possible:

Time Out: Where were you?

Tune In: How did you release?

Turn On: Did you discover anything new?

....

....

....

....

....

....

....

....

....

....

....

....

....

....

4. **Reflect:** Upon returning at a later stage and reviewing the notes you have made, what did your *Time Out, Tune In, Turn On* experience reveal?

 Were you able to release the issue that was bothering you?

 How did this feel?

 Did you receive wise guidance?

 Have you begun to heal?

 Is there anything new that you will be doing for yourself?

....

....

....

....

....

....

....

....

....

....

....

Everyday Situation

5. **Record:** Were you able to apply *Time Out, Tune In, Turn On* in an everyday life situation today? A record of your experience is invaluable. Try to record your experience during each stage of *Time Out, Tune In, Turn On* with as much detail as possible:

Time Out: What did you do? Where did you go?

Tune In: How did you release? What did you have access to?

Turn On: Did you discover anything new?

....

....

....

....

....

....

....

....

....

....

....

....

....

6. **Reflect:** Upon returning at a later stage and reviewing the information you have recorded, what do you notice?

Has continual outpouring developed as a pattern in your life?

Do you make space and time in your life to give inwardly?

What does self-love encompass for you?

Are you doing anything different in your life?

Do you feel a deeper connection with your precious heart?

....

....

....

....

....

....

....

....

....

....

....

....

Creations

Creations

Chapter 15

Sneaky Source of Pain

Everyday Experience IV

1. Journal

I sit in my garden contemplating my issues with control and admit that I have lived through a lot of control, and that I have tried to control much too. Looking back, I laugh because it was so hard trying to keep it all together. The convincing arguments and statements from my mind—that this must be done and it must be done that way—have been a tiring, old pattern. They have also been such a heavy burden.

Take for instance, pizza making. My husband offered to make bacon and banana pizzas for dinner one evening during an early stage of our relationship. I thought I was open and quite curious. This was a combination that I had never tried. I was rather surprised to discover this, since during my childhood, I had grown up in the garden and experienced a wide range of fresh, organic pickings, textural sensations, and flavour combinations. My family didn't do bacon and banana pizzas though, and in all honesty, whilst interesting, this combination sounded far too simple.

My family's approach was to pile it on, perhaps with too much good intention and generosity, and getting lost amidst it all. Our pizza sauce, when we made it as children, was always tomato paste enhanced with garlic and oregano, and balanced with a little sugar and salt. So, whilst I was eager to try my husband's unique, yet simple flavour combination, I insisted that I teach him my family's tomato paste recipe. For a number of years now, Saturday night has been "pizza night," and bacon and banana is our favourite combination.

However, over the recent months, when I had made other types of pizzas using pita bread or homemade dough bases, I found myself slipping out of sheer production pressure. To compensate, on a number of occasions, I had used the tomato paste straight from the bottle! How dare !! I felt guilty about this and tried to keep it a secret the first few times. Eventually my truth came out!

Last Saturday, my husband did the "easy way" and owned up after I had eaten half and complimented him. It really did taste delightful. In hindsight, the undertones of garlic in my family's version of tomato sauce were just too overpowering for the delicate blend of bacon and banana.

I had a sinking realisation that he really did know best at first and his "own way" was perfectly fine. Yet, I interfered and controlled. Whilst this might be a short story, my control pattern has taken four years to surface and dissolve.

How subtle a sneaky source of pain can infiltrate our lives! I'm on the lookout, so beware sneaky, controlling ways!

2. Reflection

Slipping up and owning up is a humbling process. Control can be a tough pattern of pain to confront and release, especially when patterns are established in childhood. Well, so I thought. By being real and "cutting myself some slack," I was able to cut myself free from the heavy bind that that I thought was held over me since I was a child. It was a bind of my subconscious mind, still trying to have a hold over me and trying to have a hold over others using the disguise of a well-intentioned adult.

Pizza sauce isn't the only control pattern of mine—I've been a control freak! The up side is, now that I've confronted control, I can let it go and feel the ease that comes with living free. I used to wonder, how does it feel to live free of control, to embrace spontaneity and synchronicity?

The inner wisdom of my heart tells me that we all have unique talents and special gifts to offer. But we also need "space" to explore and then share. We need to get out of each other's way and provide space for living freely. In this way we can ignite the magic of life, experiment with ideas, create new pathways, and ultimately present unique gifts of surprise! This is real, joyful living—it's how we feel alive!

I am grateful for having used Time Out, Tune In, Turn On the evening my husband came clean. Instead of shutting him out or pinning him down to protect my sneaky secret and controlling ego,

I also decided to "come clean." Rather than fight the battle of blame, we sat together in silence, looked at one-another, smiled with forgiveness, and knew that we could create a new way.

My husband and I took time out together that evening. We were both present, still, soft, and quiet. I was embarrassed and saddened, and felt plain lousy that I insisted he make pizza sauce "my way," for all that time. My husband was aware of my feelings and sat silent, gracefully providing space for humble acceptance. Together, we realised that succumbing to control for the sake of pleasing of one-another, has been a pattern that has gone on for too long in our relationship. We awakened to this sneaky source of pain and its welcome release was intimate and liberating.

Embarrassing laughs and cheeky scolds were a light way to tune-in and experience mutual release. Together, we came clean and offered one-another much needed space for a fresh start. We vowed to strengthen our inner courage and simply do as we desire, without interfering or attempting to control each other's creativity—no hard rules or trying to please. We gave one-another permission to ask for space and to give a gentle nudge when an old pattern of domineering control was looming, ready to creep its way back in.

We united through mutual healing in the heart-of-the-moment. There was a subtle buzz in the air, a sense that the vibration of our beings was lifted through mutual acknowledgement and honouring of the goodness and purity of our hearts. We wanted to embrace one-another with whole-hearted love, to discover our uniqueness and creative flare, to express our individuality, and to nurture our spirits with generosity.

Our process of forgiveness was discrete but complete. Coupled with mutual release, we supported each other's healing and experienced a simple yet profound everyday life change. We felt reassured that our relationship would blossom through love. Our awareness of the necessity to offer one-another space to live and create freely was renewed.

Bring your shadow side to the light.

Love and space create
blossoming relationships.

Free your heart and fill your life
with goodness.

Discover your uniqueness &
share your talents. Invite magic into your life!

Reader's Journal

Visualisation

1. **Recall:** Can you recall a situation in which you have tried to influence another person or tried to control? Would you consider talking with this person to wipe your slate clean?

....

....

....

....

....

....

....

....

....

....

....

....

....

....

....

....

....

....

....

2. **Visualise:** Close your eyes. Imagine that you sensitively ask this person if they would like to experience mutual healing using *Time Out, Tune In, Turn On*:

Time Out: See yourself feeling centred and at peace. Approach this person with sensitivity.
Let them know that you would like to come clean about something.
Ask if they would feel comfortable taking a moment with you in a quiet private space.

Tune In: Release.
Say what you need to.
If this is too much for you, consider writing down all that you need to say and then give it to the person to read.
Let the process of release flow naturally for you.
Provide time and space for the other person to also release all that they need to, in the way that flows naturally for both of you.

Turn On: Once your releasing is complete and the other person's releasing is also complete, remain in silence.
Stillness and silence is necessary at times.
Breathe and simply be.
Connect within.
Rest in the safe space of your heart.
Feel at ease and experience peace.
Trust that all that needs to happen here will occur as it needs to at the time.
When you both feel ready, offer thanks.
Go on with your life in peace.

3. **Record:** Write about your experience in applying *Time Out, Tune In, Turn On* with another person during visualisation with as much detail as possible:

Time Out: What did you say to this person? Where did you both go?

Tune In: How did you release and how did you feel?
Did the other person also release?
How did they respond?
Were you able to provide space and time to allow this process to complete?

Turn On: Were you able to feel at peace in the safe space of your heart?
Did you experience mutual peace?
How did your heart guide you in this situation?

....

....

....

....

....

....

....

....

....

....

4. **Reflect:** Upon returning at a later stage and reviewing the notes you have made, what did your visualisation and mutual healing experience reveal?

    Did you see yourself behaving differently?

    Were you able to create shared heart space for mutual healing with the other person?

    Has your relationship with this person changed?

    How have you grown?

    ....

    ....

    ....

    ....

    ....

    ....

    ....

    ....

    ....

    ....

    ....

    ....

    ....

Everyday Situation

5. **Record:** Were you able to apply *Time Out, Tune In, Turn On* in an everyday life situation today? A record of your experience is invaluable. Try to record your experience during each stage of *Time Out, Tune In, Turn On* with as much detail as possible:

Time Out: What did you say or do? Where did you go?

Tune In: How did you release? What did you use?

Turn On: Did you discover anything new?

....

....

....

....

....

....

....

....

....

....

....

....

....

....

6. **Reflect:** Upon returning at a later stage and reviewing the information you have recorded, what did your everyday experience in using *Time Out, Tune In, Turn On* reveal?

Are you becoming aware that you may be exercising control or trying to influence other people?

Have you started to come clean about any other issues?

How do you feel upon releasing control?

Are you forgiving yourself?

Are you accepting forgiveness from others?

Can you feel how release of control in relationships opens the gateway for mutual life change?

Are you giving yourself more space and time for creativity?

Has anyone surprised you with an unexpected offering lately?

....

....

....

....

....

....

....

....

....

Creations

Creations

Chapter 16

Magic Mop

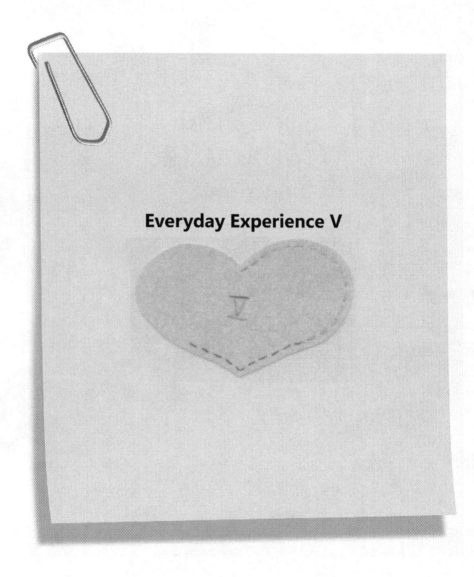

Everyday Experience V

1. Journal

It was time for breakfast and our usual saga was about to be underway. We woke early. Blessed with a beautiful garden, we enjoyed spending a precious early hour or so outside. Understandably, we were reluctant to move toward the home for breakfast. Reality set in and I began to wonder: How can this transition be a little smoother?

Yesterday I brought breakfast out to the garden and feast we did, as we had worked for ninety minutes solid. Little did I know that we'd go on for another ninety minutes more! Fortunately, it was Sunday and we were able to embrace the flow of our desires. We had no schedule to stick to for school and puppy was happy to dig holes instead of going on an early-morning walk.

Today was different. I wanted to walk with my son and "Big Sis" down to the school bus and come home along the forest. We would take time to have a picnic on the bridge and count the scrub turkeys along the way. The fish in the pond would have grown as they were only babies the other week.

Naturally, I assumed our usual school-morning challenge by asserting, "Okay, it's time to go inside." I asked Big Sis to set the table and this meant that my little one needed to pull at my nightie, bang on the wall, play ball with puppy, and pull out our personal files. When Big Sis was home on a Monday morning, the dynamic of three was far different from just the two of us.

Intensity set in; my voice firmed with direct requests. I noticed my little one fleeting between activities and then he was finally willing to come to the table so we could eat together. He was happy to put a fancy strawberry ice cube in his glass of orange juice. Just as he was sitting down, he was no sooner back to the fridge for fizz and chocolate milk. I noticed while I was at the bench top. I breathed and reasoned: At least he has come up to eat!

Just as I came to the table to eat, I rushed back to get my juice and noticed spots of muddy paw prints all over the floor! I had vacuumed and mopped yesterday, a task that took well over one hour of concentrated, dedicated effort—not to mention it was in the heat! I was silently content with the illusion that clean floors painted as a foundation of composure for our home, even if they were barely noticed by the some of the people who lived here. I took a deep breath—chaos was back again. I knew I could fume. In the past, I would have reacted with a high-pitched, angry outburst.

This time, I took in a deep breath. On the out breath, I simply stated what I saw: "Oh, my gosh! There's muddy paw prints all over the clean floor!" Exclaiming just like a well-practised school teacher was partly to raise attention and partly to calm the frenzy inside me. But, with a tone of surprise and edge of lightness, I quickly sighed and said, "Well, that's easy fixed later. Let's enjoy our breakfast now." I have never said anything like this in my home before. As a child, I was brought up to clean up the mess straight away. There was no choice to opt-in, opt-out, or determine how. My early days were dominated with control and fear of consequence.

Fear has held me as a captive slave for far too long. In this instance, I decided to change and adopt a new attitude of cool contentment. My mind was particularly bothered, but I felt satisfied and rather accomplished that I could surprise the children in this way.

I've been so overly tense and hardworking for their hearts' liking. They long for me to lighten-up. Life through a child's eye is so in-the-moment, and I have known for some time that I have needed to change; to have my children seeing more of the real me rather than the "mum who dutifully does." I was doing to please, but to please whom? Certainly not them, nor me!

So after breakfast, my little one was "up and off" as usual. I was about to get the mop and clear away the mud as it was, after all, my responsibility. Yet something again shifted inside and out came another uplifting suggestion: "Let's get the magic mop!"

Heads turned, and eyes lit up! My little one followed me immediately to the laundry. He brought out the mop and I followed, singing, "Watch the magic mop, clear the muddy paw prints, out of the way!"

Well, this was a site to behold! My three-year-old son, industrious indeed, had his older, teenage sister watching with surprise as he mopped up the muddy paw prints independently. He was enjoying the entire process and feeling most delighted and satisfied with his efforts. Shifts in my life were indeed occurring. Big Sis and I were stunned!

The mud disappeared before my eyes without me lifting a finger or raising my voice. This was nice—more please! My faith in this way of living and style of parenting was renewed.

With gratitude, I rest happy in my heart that I am always learning. It is possible to shift; to change; to embrace and enjoy life as it comes! I have to remember to alter my perception, shake off my old habits and belief patterns, and toss them out with my basket of my pain.

As fleeting as these moments are, they are no less significant. I am looking forward experiencing more frequent moments like these. It's not necessarily a complete life makeover but it's a gradual becoming of a life that is more enjoyable to live. It is supported by my growing awareness and willingness to lighten-up and be reassured by the spontaneity that flows naturally, when we "turn on."

2. Reflection

I know I am healing and growing when I experience the thrill of spontaneous surprise—unexpected, delightful events that synchronise. My husband and children love seeing me free and happy. My husband wasn't home on the morning of our "magic mop" experience, but he knows all about it—this story is his favourite!

To have a sudden shift in perspective and a complimentary shift in attitude during a confronting situation that could easily escalate into a party of pain, is a new skill that I am developing from my practise of Time Out, Tune In, Turn On. My application of this strategy has become so delicate and speedy that I am now navigating around life's little hang-ups and painful spats so gracefully.

A deep breath and acknowledgement of my unique reality, in the heart of a challenging moment, is all that I need at times, to centre myself in the loving, peaceful space of my heart. This strategy is working magic in my life! I no longer have to remove myself completely from the situation or do any form of dramatic releasing. My healing and shifting are naturally occurring, in-the-moment, at the scene. I am growing on the spot and feel self-confident with my lighter, brighter attitude. I am surprising myself and other people in my life!

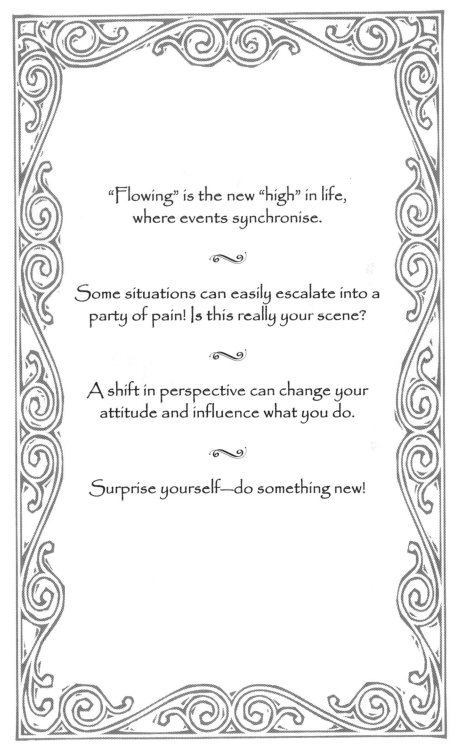

"Flowing" is the new "high" in life,
where events synchronise.

Some situations can easily escalate into a
party of pain! Is this really your scene?

A shift in perspective can change your
attitude and influence what you do.

Surprise yourself—do something new!

Reader's Journal

Visualisation

1. **Reflect:** Can you describe a recent situation where you surprised yourself with a shift in perception or attitude?

2. **Visualise:** Close your eyes. See yourself in this situation. Were you applying *Time Out, Tune In, Turn On* instinctively?

Time Out: Did you need to take a moment for yourself within the situation, to breathe and simply be?

Tune In: Did you need to do much to release? What did you do?
Were you able to accept your reality?
Did you experience relief?

Turn On: Did you need to rest in the safe space of your heart?
Were you living in-the-moment, from this centred space?
Did you experience surprise and flowing in your life?
Were you able to express gratitude for this situation?

3. **Record:** Write about how you applied *Time Out, Tune In, Turn On* in your own, unique way during visualisation, with as much detail as possible:

Time Out: Where were you and what did you do?

Tune In: How did you release?

Turn On: Were you surprised with a swift, spontaneous shift in perception or attitude?

....

....

....

....

....

....

....

....

....

....

....

....

....

4. **Reflect:** Upon returning at a later stage and reviewing the notes you have made, what did your visualisation experience reveal?

Did you see yourself experience a shift in perception and attitude?

How did the people around you respond?

Have you surprised yourself with your ability to change?

Do you like the life you are beginning to create?

Everyday Situation

5. **Record:** Were you able to apply *Time Out, Tune In, Turn On* in an everyday life situation today? A record of your experience is invaluable. Try to record your experience during each stage of *Time Out, Tune In, Turn On* with as much detail as possible:

Time Out: What did you say or do? Where did you go?

Tune In: How did you release? What did you use?

Turn On: Did you discover anything new?

....

....

....

....

....

....

....

....

....

....

....

....

....

6. **Reflect:** Upon returning at a later stage and reviewing the information you have recorded, what did your everyday experience in using *Time Out, Tune In, Turn On* reveal?

   Do you notice any changes in how you now apply this strategy?

   Are surprises flowing into your life?

   Are events synchronising?

   Are you feeling better overall?

   Are your relationships becoming lighter and more engaging?

   Are you experiencing any other elements of life change that have emerged unexpectedly?

....

....

....

....

....

....

....

....

....

Creations

Creations

Chapter 17

Lighter Living

Everyday Experience VI

1. Journal

"What are you laughing about, Mum?" I had another chuckle and my little one repeated, "What are you laughing about, Mum?"

I replied, "I don't really know!" I chuckled again and said, "Hey, at least I'm happy and laughing!" Happiness was here at last! This feeling was even more vibrant, for it arrived by surprise as I was in the middle of a number two!

My little one came in through the sliding door with his dad's shaving cream smeared across his tummy and mingled through his fingers. I closed my eyes and breathed. He knew what this action was now: "Mum's in-the-moment time out."

I didn't need to let anything out, except for a vibrant, high-pitched statement with a smile, "Hey, you keep going! I'll slide the door and we can both have some space!"

This was great, he continued and I completed.

So here I am, laughing again as I write. And, my little one is asking the same question again, "What are you laughing about, Mummy?" I continued to chuckle.

2. Reflection

In-the-moment healing works! I could have reacted and freaked out about not having my space to do a basic human bodily function, and I could have fretted out about the state of my little one's hands and his dad's empty can of shaving cream. I've done it in the past, despite my deep wish that I could have managed with more composure.

There was no freaking out this time, just time out. A pure, simple deep breath was my way to tune in, while I closed my eyes. My tune-in was rather unremarkable. Feeling quickly at ease, I turned-on and connected, with peaceful acceptance, in my heart. Here, it was easy for me to see the bright side of this situation. I knew instantaneously that we needed our space and privacy to continue and complete. There was no resistance, control, or reactivity. There were no hang-ups or further problems. We got back to doing what we needed to do and were both satisfied in having our own space, feeling fulfilled.

I completed. My little one needed more time to complete his experience, and when he was done, he was happy to wash off and watch the bubbles float away. We both came through this situation feeling complete, and shining new. I would never have envisioned that I could respond with such graceful spontaneity in such a situation! I was proud of myself and delighted with my progress. I could feel myself beginning to renew. My life was changing shape, becoming shiny, fresh, and free—just how it should be!

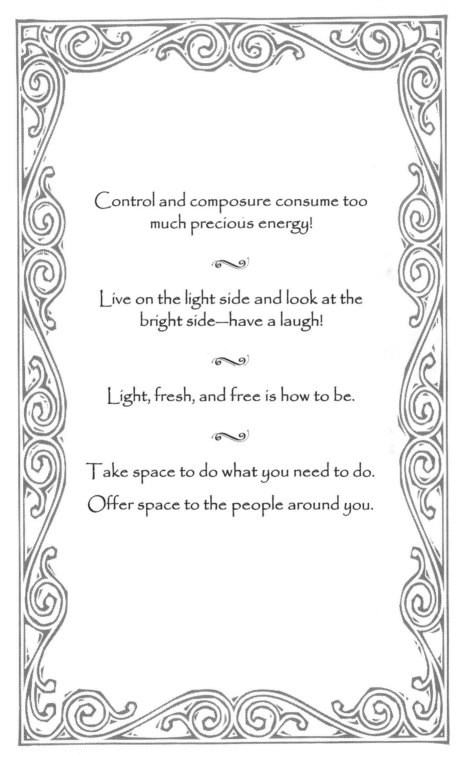

Control and composure consume too much precious energy!

Live on the light side and look at the bright side—have a laugh!

Light, fresh, and free is how to be.

Take space to do what you need to do. Offer space to the people around you.

Reader's Journal

Visualisation

1. **Recall:** Can you describe a recent situation where you surprised another person with a light, fresh, spontaneous comment or response?

....

....

....

....

....

....

....

....

....

....

....

....

....

....

....

....

....

....

....

2. **Visualise:** Close your eyes. See yourself in this situation. Did you apply *Time Out, Tune In, Turn On* spontaneously and swiftly, or were you simply turned-on?

Time Out: Did you need to take a brief moment for yourself within the situation, or was time out not necessary?

Tune In: Were you able to release quickly and easily?

Turn On: Was it a natural instinct for you to connect with your heart?
Were you able to stay turned-on?
Could you offer space for yourself and the other person to make a fresh start?
Were you able to receive and appreciate wise guidance from your heart?
Did you flow on with your life happy and in peace?

---

3. **Record:** Write about your experience in applying *Time Out, Tune In, Turn On* during visualisation in your own, unique way with as much detail as possible:

Time Out: What did you do?

Tune In: How did you release?

Turn On: Did you discover anything new?

4. **Reflect:** Upon returning at a later stage and reviewing the notes you have made, what do you notice about the way you now apply *Time Out, Tune In, Turn On*?

    Are you behaving differently, in unexpected, healthy ways?

    Are you able to accept situations as they arise?

    Are you offering other people understanding and space?

    Were you able to trust and flow with the guidance you received from your heart?

    ....

    ....

    ....

    ....

    ....

    ....

    ....

    ....

    ....

    ....

    ....

    ....

    ....

    ....

Everyday Situation

5. **Record:** Were you able to apply *Time Out, Tune In, Turn On* in an everyday life situation today? A record of your experience is invaluable. Try to record your experience during each stage of *Time Out, Tune In, Turn On* with as much detail as possible:

Time Out: What did you say or do? Where did you go?

Tune In: How did you release? What did you use?

Turn On: Did you discover anything new?

....

....

....

....

....

....

....

....

....

....

....

....

....

....

6. **Reflect:** Upon returning at a later stage and reviewing the information you have recorded, what did your everyday experience in using *Time Out, Tune In, Turn On* reveal?

- Are you now able to apply *Time Out, Tune In, Turn On* gracefully, in a variety of situations?

- Are you surprising yourself with light, spontaneous manoeuvres?

- Do you notice that you are living free from pain, control, reactivity, and resistance?

- In what other ways is your life beginning to change?

- Are you discovering new desires?

- Are you meeting your needs whilst providing other people space to meet their own needs too?

- Are you living in alignment with the path of your heart?

....

....

....

....

....

....

....

....

....

....

Creations

Creations

Chapter 18

Smoother Sailing

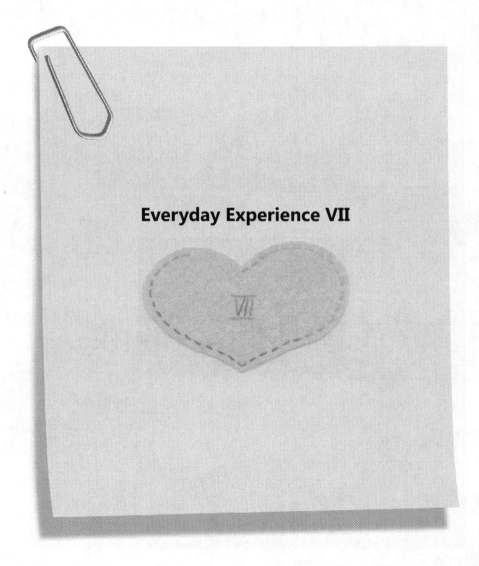

Everyday Experience VII

1. Journal

I'm exhausted, having completed six runs to and from the car to bring in the boxes and bottles. Cereal packets and nappies fell from the tall towers I stacked on both arms. I had to stack because I forgot my bags for grocery shopping and I only felt comfortable taking four boxes.

Yet, I'm laughing and feeling so blessed with a good, happy life. I asked seven people to go in front of me as I unloaded my full trolley at the supermarket. They were hesitant yet delighted to receive an unexpected kind offer. A lovely new gentleman on the register needed some friendly reassurance. He said, "I'm so tired. I've only got short arms!" I replied, "Yeah, but at least they scan fast!" Smiles, laughs, appreciation, and happy chatter were on the agenda before the school pick-up rush. The shop was busy, but it had a good vibe.

As I'm loading the shopping from the car to the kitchen, my little one has a three-kilogram bag of baby red onions all over the floor. Normally, I wouldn't buy so many, but I was fortunate to pay fifty cents for them at a market stall. The baby onions and their slippery red skins were in middle of the doorway—right where I had to walk in and out twelve or more times!

He was putting them in a wooden cable roll and rocking it from side to side while saying, "Look at them mixing, Mummy. They're making sour cream!"

My eyebrows raised and my cheeks lifted. I couldn't help but breathe in, nod, and smile. I was amused and delighted. I knew I would be okay if I tiptoed my way. We were happy!

2. Reflection

Children get on with things and "do," totally consumed by the wonder of moment. They don't over-think; they just "get on with it" and "do."

We have much to learn from their ways. Why do we jump into judgement and control, and interfere with their world so much? Why do we turn-off and tune-out from their world under the illusion that "our work" is more important? Their "play" is their work. It is important too, yet it often goes unrecognised and unappreciated in the midst of our busy day.

How different would our lives be if we appreciated the ways of our children regularly? If we took time out to watch them with wonder and delight in their creativity? I still laugh when I read this story and am so glad that I witnessed my son playing freely, with pleasure in the "now." I'm so glad that I didn't distract him or ask that he help me unpack the groceries instead of play.

I had no need for a survival strategy here. My life was busily afloat with vibrant activity, just as rays of sunshine tickle the surface of the sea. I was able to slip my way past the lingering hooks of old painful patterns, awaiting my sleepy offer of bait to surge forward. I simply got on with doing what needed to be done whilst appreciating the magnificent, bubbling alchemy around me.

My lightness of being enabled me to "flow." I sailed through the peak-hour rush at the register and navigated through the baby-onion parade, with their slippery skins lining the doorway. I needed to be ever-alert, and aware of sailing with the flow of activities in my sea of life that afternoon. I was surprised that I could live this way, bringing in such a full load. I was so surprised, I had to write about it!

My son's creativity left me feeling so refreshed. My loving heart and loving eyes helped me stay afloat of the chaos and learn a little more about myself, whilst appreciating his imagination and ingenuity. I longed to free myself of duty and slink into my desires. I really needed to kick back with a cold drink. But, in my adult world, freedom needed to be balanced with logic—ice cream needed the freezer first and then cold food needed the fridge. My refreshing cold drink would come in at third place, albeit well-deserved!

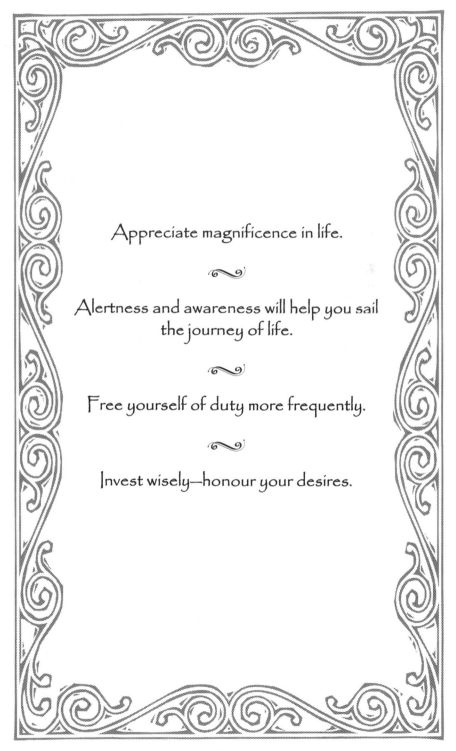

Appreciate magnificence in life.

Alertness and awareness will help you sail
the journey of life.

Free yourself of duty more frequently.

Invest wisely—honour your desires.

Reader's Journal

Visualisation

1. **Recall:** Can you describe a recent experience where you sailed through a busy situation?

2. **Visualise:** Close your eyes. See yourself in this situation. Were you using *Time Out, Tune In, Turn On* instinctively? Or, were you simply tuned-in, aware of your relationship with your surrounds, and turned-on, balancing your duties and desires?

> **Time Out:** Did you need to take a moment for yourself to observe what was occurring in this situation?
> Or, did this situation flow naturally and spontaneously?

> **Tune In:** Did you need to release during this busy experience, in order to flow with the events that you encountered along your way?
> Were you alert and tuned-in to your surrounds?
> What did you notice?
> What did you appreciate?
> Could you express gratitude for this experience amidst the chaos?

> **Turn On:** Did you feel centred in your heart?
> Did you feel at peace with your surrounds?
> Were you able appreciate the ways of other people and offer them space to be free to meet their needs?
> Were you aware of old patterns of pain?
> Were you able to appreciate your role and stay focussed?
> Were you able to gracefully accept the nature of this situation?

3. **Record:** Write about your observation of how you applied *Time Out, Tune In, Turn On* during visualisation with as much detail as possible:

Time Out: Where were you?

Tune In: Did you release tension or emotions whilst you were on the go in order to gracefully flow?
Were you able to tune-in to your surrounds and accept the flow of events that were going on around you?

Turn On: Were you centred in your heart or did you need to rest and connect to balance your needs and desires gracefully?

....

....

....

....

....

....

....

....

....

....

....

....

4. **Reflect:** Upon returning at a later stage and reviewing the notes you have made, what are you learning about your everyday life change?

   Is it new for you to "go with the flow" in a busy situation?

   Are you noticing that you can take a moment to check-in with yourself to see if you are tuned-in and turned-on within a situation quite easily?

   Are you developing heightened awareness of yourself and your surrounds?

   Has your tune-in experience evolved? Whilst we need to release tension and emotion regularly, are you noticing that you can now tune-in to express gratitude and blessings?

   Can you see yourself making different decisions and experiencing smoother outcomes?

   ....

   ....

   ....

   ....

   ....

   ....

   ....

   ....

Everyday Situation

5. **Record***:* Were you able to apply *Time Out, Tune In, Turn* On in an everyday life situation today? A record of your experience is invaluable. Try to record your experience during each stage of *Time Out, Tune In, Turn On* with as much detail as possible:

Time Out: How did you do this?

Tune In: What did you release and express?

Turn On: What did you discover when you were connected with your heart?

....

....

....

....

....

....

....

....

....

....

....

....

6. **Reflect:** Upon returning at a later stage and reviewing the information you have recorded, what do you notice about the way you use *Time Out, Tune In, Turn On*?

Are your habits and patterns of pain subsiding?

Do you now release tension and emotion when you feel that you need to?

Are you accepting the natural flow of events in your life?

How do you balance your duties and desires?

Do you feel that you are now living in a new way?

Are you becoming graceful and creative?

Are you offering other people space to express themselves freely?

Are you feeling more centred in your heart?

Are you beginning to contemplate the deeper meaning of your life?

....

....

....

....

....

....

....

....

....

Creations

Creations

Chapter 19

Flowing and Fulfilment

Everyday Experience VIII

1. Journal

I'm doing more things I desire to do and I'm becoming less critical of my surrounds. Personal fulfilment through living the path of my heart is like a melting sensation on my shoulders—I no longer feel so burdened.

I was striding down the hallway to my bedroom to change and realised, "Hey, I'd love another coffee." Without contemplation or hesitation, I turned around, enjoying a brief thrill as I whirled. My slippers facilitated easy, free spin. This was freedom in-the-moment—flowing with my desire and experiencing a vibrant, fulfilling feeling. I put the kettle on and in no time, my coffee was ready to enjoy.

"What are you doing, Mum?" asked my little son.

I noticed his sudden interest and wondered, "Is he attracted to this magical moment of mine?"

"Writing," I responded.

"Can you play?" he asked. Without hesitation, I replied, "Yes. I'll bring my coffee—I'd love to play!"

2. Reflection

As I reflect on this piece of writing, I still get a subtle, freaky feeling—I cannot believe this is me!

I still have an imprint of a heavy overlay from my old pain, and habitual pattern of resistance and reactivity. It has over-ruled my natural, joyful, loving way of living for a long, long time.

In my "old way," I would have been sneaking off to my bedroom to get dressed in a hurry. I would have held-off on my desire for a coffee because I was planning to do something else on the run. My mind would have been three steps ahead of my body. If I was just about to sit down and take a break, I wouldn't have been so willing to give it up to play with my son.

This situation was a delightful experience as my new reality. Alas, I am in the midst of everyday life change—learning, healing, growing, and loving it! I am renewing my being and reshaping my life! It is these little details that count. They matter to me, and they might interest you, so I had to write about it!

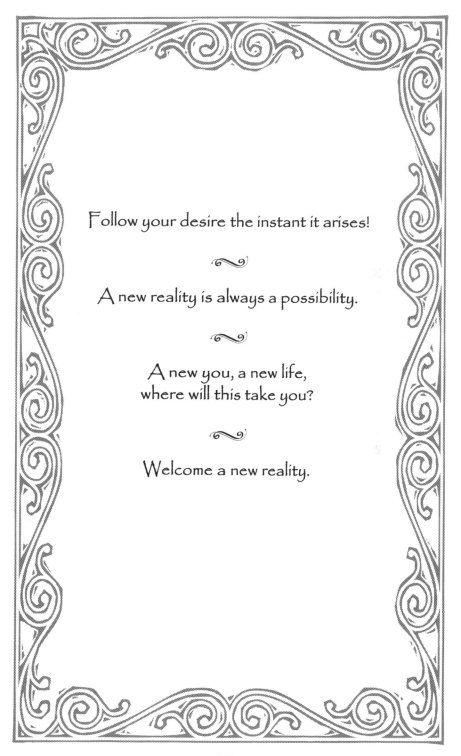

Follow your desire the instant it arises!

A new reality is always a possibility.

A new you, a new life,
where will this take you?

Welcome a new reality.

Reader's Journal

Visualisation

1. **Recall:** Can you describe a recent situation where you experienced flowing and fulfilment? Or, a situation where you know you could have slowed down?

....

....

....

....

....

....

....

....

....

....

....

....

....

....

....

....

....

....

2. **Visualise:** Close your eyes. See yourself in this situation. Were you using *Time Out, Tune In, Turn On* instinctively? Or, were you simply tuned-in to your body and environment, and turned-on, living from your heart?

Time Out: Did you take time out for yourself in a different way, perhaps with another person to have a break or create?

Tune In: Were you able to observe and appreciate the flow of events and the fulfilling sensations around you?

Turn On: Were you able to express gratitude for living in alignment with your heart?
Is this something that you would like to experience more often?
Did you feel at peace whilst also feeling more alive?

3. **Record:** Write about your experience in applying *Time Out, Tune In, Turn On* during visualisation with as much detail as possible:

Time Out: Were you able to take a moment to appreciate the events that were occurring around you?
Did you need to take time out or did this process occur swiftly and naturally for you?

Tune In: What did you appreciate about this situation?
Could you feel that you were tuned-in, alert and aware of your feelings and actions in this situation?

Turn On: Were you centred in your heart?
Could you feel that you were turned-on in-the-moment, living from your heart?

....

....

....

....

....

....

....

....

....

....

....

4. **Reflect:** Upon returning at a later stage and reviewing the notes you have made, what did your visualisation experience reveal?

- Are you surprising yourself with the scope of choices you have in your life?

- Have you noticed that you are making new and different decisions?

- Are you living in-tune with the magical beauty of life around you?

- Are you living in alignment with the path of your heart?

- Are other people drawn to being around you?

- Does your life and future feel vibrant and full of potential?

- Are you feeling fulfilled?

....

....

....

....

....

....

....

....

....

....

....

Everyday Situation

5. **Write:** Were you tuned-in and turned-on during an everyday life situation today? A record of your experience is invaluable. Try to record your experience in as much detail as possible:

....

....

....

....

....

....

....

....

....

....

....

....

....

....

....

....

6. **Reflect:** Upon returning at a later stage and reviewing the information you have recorded, what did your everyday experience in using *Time Out, Tune In, Turn On* reveal?

How is your life changing?

Are you feeling more alive?

Are you experiencing renewal—the becoming of a new you?

Are you noticing surprise and synchronicity in your life?

Has anything new been drawn to you?

Are you reshaping your life?

....

....

....

....

....

....

....

....

....

....

....

Creations

Creations

Summary

U pon completion of this book, I return to the preface and contemplate my question, which I presented then as unresolved: *Why do I find something I love and want to do so challenging at times?* I experience a strange sensation, for this question and its ironic nature, no longer bother me.

I compassionately accept that challenges will flow into my life every day, but I have now learnt to flow with the rise and fall of my emotions and to navigate smoothly through the surprises and chaotic situations that float into my environmental sea.

I live with heightened awareness of how I feel, emotionally and physically. I trust the guidance of my heart with the choices I make and give other people space to do the same. I make time to play and create, and to release my thoughts and feelings when I have the need. I give myself time and space daily, to rest in the sanctuary of my heart. Most importantly, I trust that my heart will illuminate my way, as I walk my path, learning, healing, and growing, bit-by-bit, day-by-day.

I am content. I feel alive. I now
live the path of my heart.

Conclusion

By inviting this book into your presence, I hope that you have discovered and experienced how you can live the path of your heart in everyday life and stay true to what is important to you.

I encourage you to celebrate your life change and share your journey of awakening. The changes we make day-by-day are small, yet significant, for over time, they create profound results.

I wish you all the very best in life and encourage you to embrace your unique, self-guided ability to explore your heart's path in a gentle way. I am extremely grateful to have had the opportunity to share my story of life change with you and offer a lasting, graceful blessing.

With love and peace,
Leeny.

Feel your desires.
Trust your guidance.
Live the path of your heart!

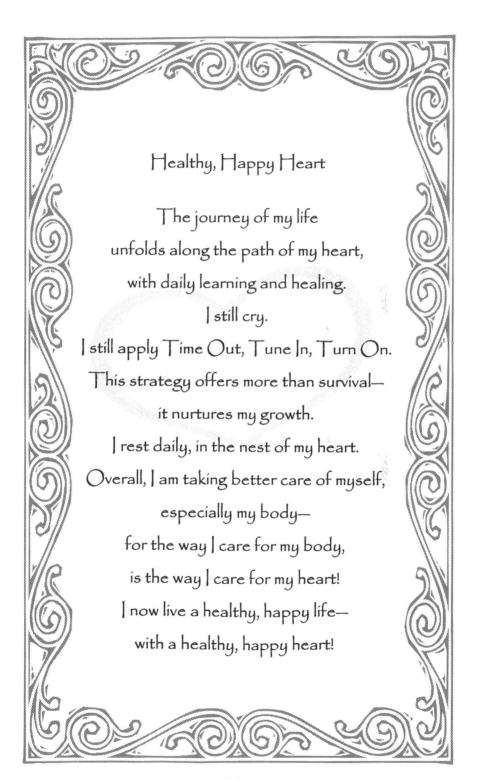

Healthy, Happy Heart

The journey of my life
unfolds along the path of my heart,
with daily learning and healing.
I still cry.
I still apply Time Out, Tune In, Turn On.
This strategy offers more than survival—
it nurtures my growth.
I rest daily, in the nest of my heart.
Overall, I am taking better care of myself,
especially my body—
for the way I care for my body,
is the way I care for my heart!
I now live a healthy, happy life—
with a healthy, happy heart!

A Quiz for You

In completing this book, you have received my gift.

Thank-you!

This is a little quiz for you:

Has Time Out, Tune In, Turn On been easy to do?

Could you use this strategy in a self-guided way?

Do you feel relief after welcome release?

Do you feel increased self-confidence?

Have you discovered new desires?

Have you received wise guidance?

Are you empowered to live the path of your heart?

Do you have a new outlook on life?

Have you embraced new relationships?

Have you experienced fresh opportunities?

Are you smiling and laughing more?

Are people offering you compliments?

Is your future bright?

Do you welcome the new you?

Acknowledgements

My heart and soul has been waiting at the window, ever so patiently, hoping that someday, I would fold back the curtains to let the sunshine in, and undo the latch so the cool whisper of the breeze can caress my skin, as I bring my inner beauty into being.

Life with my beautiful family is flourishing and full. Our dynamic ways stretch the emotional spectrum, from the intensity of heated situations to the blissful sensations of pure glee when we play carefree.

My family feeds my growth and I am deeply grateful for the love, learning, and healing that we share. I would like to say a special thank-you to the following people:

> Peter, my husband, co-creates the foundation of our happy home and vibrant family life, through his offering of love, commitment, and generosity. His sensitivity, warmth, and kindness keep me supple. He has known my talent and has patiently awaited my self-realisation, giving me the gift of time and space, to explore my way along the path of my heart.

> Jasper, my son, nurtures my heart and soul with unconditional love. He brings me daily teachings, laced with magical weavings of wonderment. He awakens my senses, guides me to explore, and encourages me to play. We thrive together in the garden, appreciating the beauty and cycles of life.

Our mother-son relationship has offered much to write about and reflect upon.

Molly, my stepdaughter, has sprinkled my life with flecks of surprise and adventure. Love has nurtured our relationship and grounded us in kind, caring roles. Together, we blossom through the process of creation, freeing our passion and spirit through a wild mix of artistic and adventurous activities.

I also extend deep gratitude to everyone who has shared their love, compassion, and support with me throughout life, including my parents, siblings, extended family, in-laws, friends, mentors, colleagues, and clients.

I express graceful gratitude to my angels and spirit guides for the blessings, healings, and unconditional love they offer through their radiant light, at any time of day, as they witness the unfolding of my earth life.

I also honour and appreciate my daily connection and healings I experience with my pets, crystals, Mother Earth, nature, and the heavenly energies which extend through the universe.

I offer my deepest gratitude, love, and blessings to all.

Thank-you.

Resources

M any resources have crossed my path at different stages of my life, all having an effect on my learning, healing, and spirituality at a destined time. Some of them are below.

Angelo, Jack. *Your Healing Power: A Comprehensive Guide to Channelling Your Healing Energies*. Judy Piatkus Publishers Ltd., London, UK, 1994.

Baldwin Dancy, Rahima. *You Are Your Child's First Teacher: What Parents Can Do with and for Their Children from Birth to Age Six*. Crown Publishing Group, Random House, Inc., New York, USA, 2000.

Calabrese, Adrian, PhD. *How to Get Everything You Ever Wanted: Complete Guide to Using Your Psychic Common Sense*. Llewellyn Publications, Woodbury, USA, 2006.

Chia, Mantak. *Taoist Ways to Transform Stress into Vitality: Inner Smile, Six Healing Sounds*. Universal Tao Publications, Chiang Mai, Thailand, 1985.

Chopra, Deepak. *Peace Is the Way: Bringing War and Violence to an End*. Harmony Books, London, UK, 2005.

Chopra, Deepak. *Synchro Destiny: Harnessing the Infinite Power of Coincidence to Create Miracles*. Random House Australia Pty. Ltd., London, UK, 2003.

Chopra, Deepak. *The Book of Secrets: Who Am I? Where Did I Come From? Why Am I Here*? Harmony Books, London, UK, 2004.

Chopra, Deepak. *The Path to Love: Spiritual Lessons for Creating the Love You Need*. Random House Australia Pty. Ltd., Sydney, Australia, 2000.

Emoto, Masaru. *Water Crystal Healing: Music & Images to Restore Your Well-Being*. Beyond Words Publishing, Inc., Portland, USA, 2006.

Fenton-Smith, Paul. *A Secret Door to the Universe: A Guide to Spiritual Development*. Simon & Schuster, Sydney, Australia, 1999.

Frantzis, B. K., *Opening the Energy Gates of Your Body: Gain Lifelong Vitality* (Tao of Energy Enhancement Series). North Atlantic Books, Berkeley, USA, 1993.

Hay, Louise. *You Can Heal Your Life*. Hay House Australia Pty. Ltd., Sydney, Australia, 1999.

Hawkins, David. *The Informed Vision: Essays on Learning and Human Nature*. Algora Publishing, New York, USA, 2002.

Hawkins, David, MD, PhD. *Power vs. Force: The Hidden Determinants of Human Behaviour*. Hay House Australia Pty. Ltd., Sydney, Australia. 2002.

Hendrix, Harville, and Helen LaKelly Hunt. *Receiving Love: Transform Your Relationship by Letting Yourself Be Loved*. Simon & Schuster Ltd., London, UK, 2005.

Hicks, Esther and Jerry. *The Amazing Power of Deliberate Intent: Living the Art of Allowing*. Hay House Australia, Sydney, Australia, 2008.

Hicks, Esther and Jerry. *The Astonishing Power of Emotions: Let Your Feelings Be Your Guide*. Hay House Australia, Sydney, Australia, 2006.

His Holiness the Dalai Lama. *A Simple Path*. Thorsons, London, UK, 2000.

His Holiness the Dalai Lama and Howard Cutler, MD. *The Art of Happiness: A Handbook for Living*. Hodder Headline Australia Pty. Ltd., Sydney, Australia, 1999.

Johnson, Yanling Lee. *A Woman's Qigong Guide: Empowerment through Movement, Diet, and Herbs*. Quality Books, Inc., Boston, USA, 2001.

Lane, Phil Jr., Judy and Michael Bopp, Lee Brown, and elders. *The Sacred Tree*. Lotus Press, Twin Lakes, USA, 2004.

Lorius, Cassandra. *Homeopathy for the Soul: Ways to Emotional Healing*. Thorsons, Hammersmith, London, UK, 2001.

Marlow, Mary Elizabeth. *Emerging Woman: How to Awaken the Unlimited Power of the Feminine Spirit.* Element Books Ltd., Boston, USA, 1996.

Margolis, Char. *Discover Your Inner Wisdom: Using Intuition, Logic, and Common Sense to Make Your Best Choices for Life, Health, Finances, and Relationships.* Fireside, Simon & Schuster, Inc., New York, USA, 2008.

Melchizedek, Drunvalo. *Serpent of Light: Beyond 2012: The Movement of the Earth's Kundalini and the Rise of the Female Light, 1949 to 2013.* Red Wheel/Weiser, LLC, San Francisco, USA, 2007.

Moss, Robert. *Conscious Dreaming: A Unique Nine-Step Approach to Understanding Dreams.* Crown Trade Paperbacks, New York, USA, 1996.

Myss, Caroline. *Anatomy of the Spirit: The Seven Stages of Power and Healing.* Bantam Books, Sydney, Australia, 1996.

Myss, Caroline. *Sacred Contracts: Awakening Your Divine Potential.* Bantam Books, Sydney, Australia, 2001.

Oslie, Pamala. *Love Colours: A New Approach to Love, Relationships, and Auras.* New World Library, Novato, California, USA 2007.

Palmer, Magda. *The Healing Power of Crystals: Precious Stones and Their Planetary Interactions.* Rider Books, London, UK, 1988.

Paramhans Swami Maheshwarananda. *The Hidden Power in Humans: Chakras and Kundalini.* European University Press, Vienna, Austria, 2004.

Paramhans Swami Maheshwarananda. *Yoga in Daily Life: The System: Harmony for Body, Mind, and Soul.* European University Press, Vienna, Austria, 2000.

Pitchford, Paul. *Healing with Whole Foods: Asian Traditions and Modern Nutrition.* North Atlantic Books, Berkeley, USA, 2002.

Rooney, Meredith. *I Have Found My Castle.* Boolarong Press, Brisbane, Australia. 1997.

Sha, Zhi Gang, Dr. *Divine Soul Mind Body Healing and Transmission System: The Divine Way to Heal You, Humanity, Mother Earth, and All Universes.* Atria, Simon & Schuster, Inc., New York, USA, 2009.

Simmons, Robert. *Stones of the New Consciousness: Healing, Awakening & Co-creating with Crystals, Minerals, & Gems*. Heaven and Earth Publishing, LLC, Berkeley, USA, 2009.

Smith, Penelope. *When Animals Speak: Advanced Interspecies Communication*. Beyond Words Publishing, Inc., Portland, USA, 1999.

Templeton, Rose Maree. *Numerology: Numbers and Their Influence*. Rockpool Publishing, Sydney, Australia, 2007.

Tolle, Eckhart. *A New Earth: Awakening to Your Life's Purpose*. Penguin Group, Sydney, Australia, 2005.

Tresidder, Jack. *Symbols and Their Meanings*. Duncan Baird Publishers Ltd., London, UK, 2006.

Virtue, Doreen, PhD. *Archangels and Ascended Masters: A Guide to Working and Healing with Divinities and Deities*. Hay House Australia, Pty. Ltd., Sydney, Australia, 2003.

Virtue, Doreen, PhD. *Daily Guidance from Your Angels: 365 Angelic Messages to Soothe, Heal, and Open Your Heart*. Hay House Australia, Pty. Ltd., Sydney, Australia, 2006.

Virtue, Doreen, PhD. *Healing with the Angels: How the Angels Can Assist You in Every Area of Your Life*. Hay House Australia, Pty. Ltd., Sydney, Australia, 1999.

Virtue, Doreen, PhD. *The Lightworker's Way*. Hay House Australia, Pty. Ltd., Sydney, Australia, 1997.

White, Ian. *Australian Bush Flower Essences*. Bantam Books, Australia, Sydney, Australia, 1999.

White, Ian. *Australian Bush Flower Healing*. Bantam Books, Sydney, Australia, 1999.

Zeck, Robbi. *The Blossoming Heart: Aromatherapy for Healing and Transformation*. Aroma Tours in conjunction with Brolga Publishing, Australia, 2004.